MEDITATIONS With THE HOPI

The Myth of Emergence

Meditations With™ The Hopi

Robert Boissiere

Bear & Company
Santa Fe, New Mexico

Bear & Company, Inc.
P.O. Box 2860
Santa Fe, NM 87504

Design: Mina Yamashita
Illustrations: Cynthia West
Typography: Copygraphics, Santa Fe
Printed in the United States by BookCrafters, Inc.
A limited edition of fine art prints of eight of the illustrations
in this book is available by writing: Cynthia West,
1542 Cerro Gordo Road, Santa Fe, NM 87501.

CONTENTS

HOPI INTRODUCTIONS
TO THE AUTHOR

Ferrell Secakuku:

Robert Boissiere says he is a Frenchman, but we call him Banana Clan ever since I can remember. I was about thirteen years old when I used to see him at Shipaulovi.

He did a lot of daily chores with Leslie Koyawena. Leslie was a personal friend of Robert and with his old burro they went for water, chopped wood, worked the corn in the fields, and even hunted rabbits Hopi style.

I remember him carrying his bow and arrows during one of the hunts, but I don't know if he ever shot a rabbit with it! The rest of us didn't carry bows and arrows in those days but a "hunting stick."

He often came to my father's store in Shipaulovi to chat over the village's past and also when he was in France.

The Banana Clan has a shrine north of our village of Shipaulovi and Leslie Koyawena helped him find the right location for the shrine.

Robert often teases us that someday his kachinas will come to Hopi to dance and they will bring lots of bananas for the people as a generous gesture to advocate the continued religious activities of the Hopi along with cigarettes, fruits, and other things that kachinas partake of as a symbol of the sustenance of the good life and a happy world to emerge with the eradication of hunger.

He used to say to Leslie and to my father, Hale Secakuku, and now to me that the Hopi should not ever relinquish their religious activities, as the world around them needs it.

The Banana Clan agrees with the Hopi in saying that the Hopi religion will keep the world together for a long time to come.

I personally believe that Robert's writings give a true implication or meaning of the way Hopis feel, think, and act at Shipaulovi. I further think that his books are historically important for the village of Shipaulovi and will someday serve as a documentary material for our cause. These books only portray people, his friends, and do not violate the religious aspect of the Hopi people at Shipaulovi; they should not anyway as Robert is not initiated in the Hopi religion.*

When he visits Shipaulovi, Robert still stays with Leslie's and Alta's family like Frieda and Walter. He often talks about Walter as being just like his father, Leslie, a smart and good farmer who obtains his spiritual guidance from his Hopi religion.

I asked Robert why he keeps on coming to Shipaulovi and he said to me:

"Perhaps I once was a Hopi living at Shipaulovi and of the same clan with which Leslie migrated to Hopi but I was reincarnated as a "Frenchman Banana."

Ferrell Secakuku is a member of Second Mesa Shipaulovi village and the Snake Clan. He is owner and manager of Secakuku Enterprises that manages the Hopi Cultural Center motel and restaurant along with the Second Mesa cantina and supermarket.

---

*This is to say that the author cannot in any way divulge religious secrets not being a member of a Hopi native society or clan outside of the Banana Clan, whose purpose and recognition by the village of Shipaulovi is mentioned in the last chapter and conclusion of this book.

Walter Koyawena

I want to introduce Robert Boissiere, a long-time friend of my family and of the Hopi people.

He has been a friend, an uncle, and a brother of my family and me as long as I can remember. My fondest memory of him was when he brought his French daughter named Poucette to Shipaulovi. My mother dressed her in a Hopi manta and fixed her hair in the Hopi maiden butterfly whorls so Robert could take a picture of her with us Hopi kids. We were about ten or eleven years old at the time and things went very well until Poucette began to giggle just about the time our picture was to be snapped. This giggling happened every time Robert was about to snap the picture. Anyway, our silliness got to where all of us could not help but laugh and Robert became very angry, which made us giggle even more.

I am now 43 years old but when I look at that picture today, I still cannot help laughing and this makes me happy.

Robert and my family have had many grand experiences together and this is only one of them.

Robert, the Banana Clan Man, has been a true friend of the Hopi people. I am hopeful that this book will bring no unhappiness to my people but instead a closer and better understanding of the Hopi by all mankind.

Walter Koyawena, Lomahunao, "Handsome Bear," is Leslie Koyawena's eldest son. Walter and his wife Eula teach at the Second Mesa Elementary School; like his father he is a farmer, a member of Shipaulovi village, and a member of Four Head Sun Clan.

PREFACE AND ACKNOWLEDGMENTS

Traditionally, the life of the Hopi people is divided into two main currents. One is the clan system, which regulates the physical or exoteric facets of Hopi life and the relationship of one person with another. The other is the different religious societies, mainly the Catsina cult, which binds the Hopi together through one religious experience of great strength and takes care of their esoteric needs.

Through the years, Hopi society has been scrutinized, observed, and written about by eminent scholars, perhaps more than any other Native American group, especially in the last hundred years. Spanish chronicles mention them also, but not in the same scientific manner as contemporary researchers have done. Well known among archeologists, anthropologists, ethnologists, and writers are Edward S. Curtis, Alexander M. Stephen, Jesse W. Fewkes, Adolf F. Bandelier, Frederick Webb Hodge, and more recently, Frank Waters. Indeed, many brilliant minds studied and learned about the Hopi, but very few learned *from* the Hopi.

The purpose of *Meditations With The Hopi* is to let us benefit and learn from their ancestral sources and to compare the Hopi Way with our own system of values, for they embody information of a very unique nature coming from a wise people. In no way will this book compare with the works of scholars, because its intent is to give the student of Hopi spirituality a guide, a manual, with which to learn from the Hopi.

It is important to know what the actual physical cosmos of the Hopi is, what could be called their earthly universe. It is a much larger geographical area than the actual Hopi reservation. It is an area delimited by sacred shrines. In the east, the limit is set by the ruins of their ancient villages now deep in Navajo territory around Canyon de Chelly, close to Window Rock, the Navajo capital. The northern boundary is the Kaibab Forest mountain range, which long supplied them with the logs to build their houses, wood to heat them, and wild game to feed their families. In the west, the border of this spiritual universe of the Hopi is the Grand Canyon of the Little Colorado River, where many of their most sacred shrines are located, including the mythical place of emergence of the Hopi people. A pilgrimage to this sacred spot is required of every Hopi at least once in a lifetime. Finally, the southern boundary of this earthly cosmogenic territory — in the center of which their physical life operates — is the San Francisco Mountains above Flagstaff, Arizona, which the Hopi refer to as "the San Francisco Peaks." With an elevation of 11,000 feet, these peaks are the mythical home of the Catsinas, their spirit retreat, where year after year, the masked ceremony of the year called the Niman, "going home dance," sends them at the end of July or early August. The Catsina spirits stay in the San Francisco Peaks until they reappear on top of the mesas in late November for Soyal ceremonies, reopening the Catsina year. This territorial universe is not what the bureaucracy calls the Hopi Reservation, which is much smaller, basically in the center of these four more distant boundaries.

Hopi dialect is known as "Uto Aztecan," suggesting two

geographical poles far away from each other. This could give a clue to their prehistoric past. Aztec country was in central and southern Mexico, where the Aztec empire once stood; and Ute country is in Colorado and Utah, their ancestral home. To substantiate the claim that Hopi clans could have come that far north and south, Hopi ancestral homes abound in Colorado and Utah (Mesa Verde and Hovenweep). Hopi legend mentions a legendary "Red City of the South," which the Hopi call *Palatkwapi*, or "Red House," which, according to scholars, may suggest a place where at least a clan could have migrated from a very long time ago, the place located possibly as far south as South America. This could mean that a very distant past might be available for us to know and experience through Hopi rituals, some of which have changed very little from those ancient times.

Contemplatives of the desert, the Hopi have developed over the years a discipline comparable to that practiced by other historic communities living in similar environments, such as the Essenes, who lived near the Dead Sea from 200 B.C. to A.D. 100 They were about 4,000 strong and lived with their families in fortified villages. There are also similarities with the order of the Templars, whose military know-how was put to use during the Crusades. Constantly threatened by surrounding and plundering tribes such as the Navajo, Ute, and Apache, the Hopi had to develop similar protectionist skills in order to survive in their desert environment. This monastic vision of Hopi spirituality must be understood in order to grasp their ceremonialism as well as their cultural lives, which have developed over tens of centuries. Hopi elders themselves have compared their rules to monastic ones, and quotations from them will be introduced later in the meditations.

Being influenced by the power of the right side of the

R-brain

brain, Hopi life relies mostly on intuition as opposed to logic and reason. This overwhelming use of the right-brain functions causes their minds to grasp the coming "Age of Revelation" with more certainty than most Caucasian minds.

The Hopi word, *koyaansquatsi*, expresses the way they feel about today's world, which translates as "a world out of balance." A petroglyph can be found on a huge rock near the village of Oraibi, usually referred to as *Prophecy Rock*, on which the human period in which humanity will find itself "out of balance" is vividly portrayed.

There are some similarities between Hopi and Christian spirituality. I believe that the sacrificial ritual of the eagle performed during Niman Catsina is a ritual that encompasses the Christ consciousness in its universal sense. Even though the Hopi could not have had any contact with Christian theology before the arrival of the Spaniards in the 1500s, *Kwahu*, the brother eagle, is viewed as the bridge, the intermediary, between the divine and the human, to whom prayers, offerings and special demands are made through the medium of his yearly sacrifice and prior to his departure for the realm of the Great Spirit.*

Although the physical formats are totally different, the contents of the revelation are obviously the same, which cannot be surprising when one considers that there is but one source for us all. It is no wonder the Hopis have stayed away from the Christian interpretation of the revelation when one considers that it has been with them right along in the

---

*In MesoAmerica, the so-called myth of Quetzalcoatl, with its compassionate overtones, has played a similar role in interpreting revelation for the peoples of early Central and South America, which prepared the people to accept the Christian revelation which came at a later date.

form most appropriate for them. In order for a religious channel to have its full meaning, it must relate culturally and historically to the people to become spiritually valid. Because of its Judeo-Roman roots, the Christian channel had no special meaning for the Hopi, who find in their rituals the spiritual food to sustain them.

My own arrival in the Hopi world happened in 1948 and was followed by my stay there, leading to my virtual adoption by a family of the Second Mesa village of Shipaulovi. I consider myself extremely fortunate to have known life at Hopi virtually the way it was 100 years earlier, with no paved roads, no electricity, no telephone, no running water, no public schools, and practically no automobiles. We still then ate our meals on the floor, where we also slept, and I learned how to eat corn stew without a spoon. Communications were so difficult then through sand trails that the flow of tourists was manageable, whereas now it becomes difficult to handle. Despite all the pressures brought by twentieth century communications systems, I consider it a miracle that the Hopi have retained enough of their original spirit to maintain their identity and the purity of life which they call the Hopi Way. It is my sincere wish as a writer that what this book contains will help the student of Hopi spirituality to have a clear vision of the Hopi unity of dimension, purpose, balance, and genuine faith in themselves.

Information which could in any way violate the Hopi right of privacy or the secrecy of certain rituals or ceremonies is not included in this book.

I have compiled a wealth of research and information published over the years on Hopi by scientists, writers, photographers, and some of the Hopi elders themselves, creating a synthesis of it for the purpose of introducing the profound esoteric level of Hopi life to the outside world, and attempting in this way to bring Hopi religious beliefs alongside the great religious currents of our times.

A great deal of the information contained in this book comes from statements made by Hopi spiritual leaders, elders, and chiefs during Hopi hearings called by the Hopis and conducted by a team appointed by Mr. Glenn L. Emmons, then Commissioner of Indian Affairs, from July 15 to July 30, 1955.

I have used extensively the minutes of these meetings as a unique source of information necessary to write this book. The meetings were conducted at the following villages: Hotevilla, Shungopovi, Mishongnovi, Shipaulovi, Kyakotsmovi, Bakabi, Moencopi, and First Mesa. These minutes are a unique compilation of Hopi leaders' statements made on the history, myths, legends, and religion of the Hopi. According to the Hopi leaders themselves, these hearings were held at their request in order to have an opportunity to present to the world the basis upon which their world is established.

These *Meditations With The Hopi* I dedicate to the men who urged me to be a seeker of the truth, my earthly teachers.

Professor Pierre Lecomte Du Nöuy, associate member of the Rockefeller Institute, author of *Human Destiny*.

Father Teilhard De Chardin, researcher, paleontologist, and author.

Dr. Frederick Webb Hodge, anthropologist, director of the Southwest Museum in Los Angeles, and editor of Edward S. Curtis' twenty volumes in *The North American Indian* series.

Paul Coze, philosopher, writer, art teacher, and a great friend of the Hopi.

Last but not least, Leslie Koyawena, the humble Hopi farmer whom I considered to be my brother and whose presence in my life I miss enormously.

A few months before his recall to the underworld, we spent a couple of weeks together at my home in Santa Fe. It was at that time that I put on tape the following prayer, which I asked him to teach me:

"If we really pray from our whole heart for everybody, for our people, not just for us but for the whole world that we can live good, healthy lives, the one who takes good care of us from above,* our father, he will take good care of us and will help us live in a good way.

That is what we have to pray, that is what I say in my language it is to pray."

(Leslie Koyawena's unedited prayer.)

---

*"The one who takes good care of us from above",
is the Sun and not the Christian concept of God. Hopis
are sun worshipers.

AUTHOR'S NOTE

It is important for the reader to remember that the Hopi language is a phonetic Uto-Aztecan dialect and that therefore Hopi words end up being written somewhat differently depending on who is doing it. For example, the word *catsina* is also commonly spelled *kachina*; I have chosen the first spelling, as phonetically it sounds more correct to me than the latter spelling.

It is also true that Hopi myths, legends, and stories differ somewhat from Hopi village to Hopi village, or Hopi clan to Hopi clan, although not essentially.

INTRODUCTION

On the high plateaus of the desert of Northern Arizona there is a Garden of Eden. There is no luxuriant plant growth there, as in the mythical one of Adam and Eve. Visions of rainbow colors on canyon walls, shredded faces of stone promontories, sand hills, rocks and gullies can be found in this desert country of southwestern North America. The Hopi built their homes centuries ago on top of the mesas, rocky flagships of the desert afloat on waters of sand.

Today, the Hopi are a small group of Native Americans numbering around 12,000 people, compared with the huge Navajo tribe which surrounds them on all sides. They occupied this harsh and mighty land at least as far back as 800 to 1,000 years ago, and we can still see the ruins of their ancestral villages scattered on the great desert of Utah, Colorado, Arizona, New Mexico, and part of old Mexico.

The Hopi migrations which led them to their present home might have taken 500 years or more, and this great journey is part of the Hopi sacred tradition. In the myths, legends and stories constituting the Hopi historical oral tradition, this journey is referred to as "The Migration."

The Hopi culture appears as one of the most important centers of native ceremonialism and native social organization of North America in the findings of the scientific community, the art world, and the public in general. There are a number of reasons for that. Hopi rituals and cere- monies symbolize the spirit and values of ancient America practically unaltered, in spite of 400 years of intrusion by European cultures. Of all native ceremonials, the *Catsina* cult (also *Katcina* or *Kachina*) remains perhaps the most original, despite contacts with the Spanish and Anglo-American worlds.*

Protected for so long by the immensity of the desert, the harshness of the mesa climate, the absence of roads and other communication media, the Hopi are a fascination in the public mind. More than any other group in North, Central, or South America, the Hopi have retained their aboriginal culture, with its religious expression in its purest form. And they embody a philosophy of life totally in balance with their physical and spiritual environment.

One of the greatest experiences when going to the land of Hopi — and perhaps one of the greatest experiences in life — is to witness a Catsina ceremony. In the openness of a Hopi village square (plaza), with the immensity of the desert as a backdrop, or enclosed in the sacredness of a

---

* Due to geographic isolation, Hopis as well as Zunis did not fall under Spanish influence as much as did the Pueblos of the Rio Grande River area, who after the Pueblo Rebellion of 1680, were brutally reconquered by the Spanish.

In the territories occupied by the invading Spanish forces, kivas were destroyed, sacred objects of worship desecrated, and many Indian priests killed. As a result, the Pueblo ceremonies were forced to become secretive, as most are today. Hopis and Zunis meanwhile, continued to perform Catsina dances in the open, above ground, or in the kivas accessible to visitors under certain circumstances.

Hopi kiva during the *Powamu* ceremonial, nothing is more stirring than the first sight of the half-human, half-divine Catsinas. When thirty or forty of these imposing Catsinas display the astonishing garb of part human and part animal, part bird or part star, amidst the synchronistic dancing steps and the rhythms of sacred songs, they are the centaurs of our aboriginal past.

Anyone who has been blessed by being in the presence of these ancient spirits of native America will always hold deep in the psyche this priceless experience of the continuity of the ancient rituals revealed in the present. When one experiences Catsinas pounding the earth with their dancing feet, then one knows they are always dancing. This is perhaps the reason for the attraction of the Hopi Way on people's minds—Europeans and Asiatics alike. Here in the present, uninterrupted from the depth of humanity's past, are the thoughts and beliefs that were everyone's only yesterday.

Modern Egypt, Greece, Mexico, and Peru have issued from the cultures that shaped them, but the present populations of those countries are a faint representation of their past greatness. The Europeans who settled North America have greatly distanced themselves from their aboriginal native spiritual roots. But the Native Americans, most purely represented by the Hopi of today with their ceremonies and rituals, are what they always have been, as 800-year-old petroglyphs reflect. It is the testimony of what has been our own past as re-experienced by our twentieth century selves, the past and present all as one, which is so unique at Hopi. It is this uniqueness which attracts a world bent on remembering, or rather trying to remember, its origins.

Within Hopi rituals and sacred ceremonies, the ancient knowledge of early humanity is deposited. It is brought to us without interruption or corruption. Most of us will go to Hopi driven by the force of the primeval need to be in communion with the source, even though we may not consciously recognize our need.

As in ancient days, the Hopi ceremonial calendar follows both the daily and the annual orbit of the earth around the sun, synchronizing the exoteric and esoteric facets of everyday life. In the modern industrial and technological society, necessities of physical needs seem to overwhelm the whole of life, leaving little or no time for the essential energies that are the basis of man's presence on earth. That is what essentially divides the two worlds.

In order to join in meditation with the Hopi, which is the purpose of this book, we have to be willing to enter the time/space of the daily atmosphere of ceremonial and social life of the Hopi. We can differentiate the acquired superficial outer core imposed on us by our culture and the timeless calendar of the Hopi rituals which permeates their everyday life. It is the clock that regulates the planet and its plants, animals and people, from birth to the grave, and it is a time sense we all know well deep inside.

Meditations With The Hopi will naturally unfold when one lends an attentive ear to the sound of the moccasined feet of the Catsinas pounding the floors of the kivas or the ground of the village squares, with the sound of the rattles, the bells, the drum, and the turtle shells, which are the very "breath" of their meditation.

Divided into six chapters, the following work will approach the Hopi cosmos from each of its six different levels: the Underworld, The Emergence, The Migrations, The Ceremonial Calendar, The Social Life, and The Upper World. This will provide you with a vision of Hopi consciousness. After letting you absorb the Hopi experience, each chapter will end with an overview of the subject matter of that chapter.

In order to grasp what Hopi spirituality is about, you have to remember that the Indian visualizes the mysteries of life without the need to express them consciously to anyone, even one's own self. This is a major difference from the occidental mind, which is accustomed to projecting ideas intellectually, a consciousness we inherited from our Greco-Roman past.

A diagram depicting the six levels of the Hopi world precedes the first chapter and will graphically describe how the six dimensions are integrated with each other to form the complete experience. The differences that characterize the perception of the world surrounding us made such a diagram a necessity. The Native American dimension seems strange until you visualize it. For example, Hopi spirituality should be viewed as a "group soul" rather than the collective gathering of individual ones. The different historical paths followed by the Hopi and by the western world might have something to do with that.

The American continent was isolated for so long from the rest of the world that until "discovered," the Native American world had no contacts with the European channel of evolution. The Hopi and other Native American groups which have surfaced in the twentieth century are in a sense totally unprepared. Up to the twentieth century, Hopi society developed a social system which is communal and matri-archal in character, completely isolated from differing cultures. It was a society where each individual found a purpose with the "group soul."

Through the tight bond of the clan system and the Catsina cult, each individual feeds on the collective source. In white society, things work in quite a different way, with the judgement and criticism of the political, economic, and religious establishments as the right and prerogative of the citizen. The Hopi are inclined to accept the taboos, rules, and regulations of their world without question, as they have been time tested by centuries of constant practice. This belief in a system of life handed down to them by their ancestors has helped them through time in one of the world's toughest environments except perhaps the Sahara Desert. With our more egocentric approach to our society, we might see the Hopi point of view as railroading or brainwashing their people. But the fact remains that their world view has worked for them under environmental factors different from ours, and has helped them to cope with the exigencies of a life in desert conditions. It is well for us to remember this in order to join our consciousness with theirs in meditation.

Occasionally, Hopis do react adversely to taboos handed down to them throughout the centuries. Some might even walk away from the traditional way. But as a rule, they conform, knowing instinctively that these complicated rules of behavior have been tested through time. For example, the relationship between men and women has been codified long ago into explicit roles of husband and wife, father and mother, who is responsible for what, the domestic domain versus the area outside of the home. The activities reserved for the males of the family are farming, income, and religious teaching, and the women rule the house and the activities relating to it. It all is prescribed ritually, avoiding sources of conflict. All of this was handed down from long, long ago, a formative discipline that certainly could benefit contemporary societies such as ours. As a result, the Hopi seem contented with their rules as individuals and as a people.

Then a new factor moved in, the pressure from the outside, an environmental factor the Hopi had no defense system against. The white world surrounds them on all sides, pressuring them to change their eating habits, working schedules, ceremonial calendar, and the teaching of children. Outside influences attack some of Hopi basic thought processes, and they are even territorially threatened by the powerful Navajo Nation. It creates a disastrous situation in which no one is immune to the confusion created by the dominant cultures.

For example, in Judeo-Christian doctrine, when something wrong is done, it is called a sin. Native peoples in general and the Hopi in particular do not attach such moral stigma to something done wrongly. They simply pay the price attached to it without having to experience a feeling of guilt. From the standpoint of human growth, this is far superior than the feeling of guilt attached to the concept of sin. The capital punishment of the Hopi world is ostracism, which shows the individual has cut him/herself off from the group by wrong action. Native peoples do not incorporate guilt, but they know that each wrong action hurts other people and the universe. It is easy to see why the Hopi have shunned Christianity and never permitted it on top of their sacred mesas.

To close, it is important to state that the Hopi seem to be handling the complexities of their own lives with greater ease than we are handling the problems of our own society. I attribute this to the ultimate faith the Hopi have in the societal structure handed to them by their ancestors. This faith in their system has worked up to now, and let us hope it will in the future if some of the pressures are lifted from their everyday lives. This would give them the extra chance needed to meet the exigencies of time.

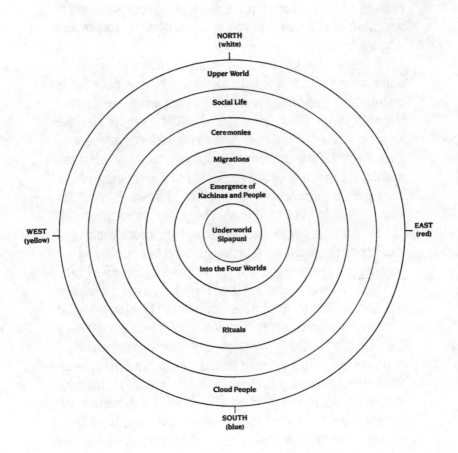

NORTH
(white)

Upper World

Social Life

Ceremonies

Migrations

Emergence of
Kachinas and People

Underworld
Sipapuni

Into the Four Worlds

Rituals

Cloud People

SOUTH
(blue)

WEST
(yellow)

EAST
(red)

1 MAS-KI:
The Underworld

TOKPELA, *The First World*

Amidst the bellowing of the volcanoes, the roaring of the
earth masses, carousing in a huge tidal wave, was the laughter
of the unchained winds, disheveled but released.
It was nature, at its best, and at its worst.
Flashes of the lightning, roaring of the thunder —
earth was being born, like a new babe, crying, demanding,
flowing in a giant faucet of lava. Like all births,
like all mutinies — it was an explosion!

Among the noises of creation, but abreast of it;
disciplining the winds, modulating their tonalities,
shaping the sounds: *Taiowa*, god of creation, spoke at last
       in a loud voice:
"I have funneled the noises of the wind,
in a powerful music of sounds," he said.
"I brought forth the dynamics of the forces of creation,
       like a work horse to its labors.
The currents of the dark lava are starting to congeal.
I need a helper, a supervisor, a foreman,
       to bring things to order."

So Taiowa, the creator, created *Sotuknang*,
and he called him his nephew. Sotuknang said:
"To make *Tokpela*, the first world, to shape these currents,
to enchain the forces unleased by Taiowa,
I need a companion, a mother to this world to come."

From the sheer power given him by the creator, Sotuknang
willed a being, a force, an energy, to give succor;
Woman Spirit, *Kokyang-Whuti,* "Spider Woman."
Together they will shape the bubbling hot and fuming mass
        called the Earth.

"Now," said Taiowa, "We have the Earth,
we have the waters to cool it, from the heat of creation.
I made the air, to coordinate the two.
So now we have the first world. But . . . no one is to be in it,
        and witness its marvels."

So, Spider Woman said:
        "Sotuknang and I thought about that."
This is how *Pokan-Hoya* and his brother, *Palongo-Hoya* came to
the first world; the twin brothers who were to look after it,
        and protect it, inhabit it.

"*Evava!*" said the first twin to his brother.
"*Ansai!*" he answered. "*Lolamai!* Everything is beautiful."
— which are the Hopi formal greetings.

Sotuknang, Spider Woman, and the twins, were created out of
the will of Taiowa to participate in the creation of mankind.
But they have to have a song to do it:
        the Song of Creation.
A song mankind shall not forget in order to survive;
a song they must keep inside of themselves,
        lest they lose the way.
It was decided the younger of the twins, *Tuvko,*
"younger brother," as they called him,
        should make the song.

The Song of Creation

From the four corners of the universe:
    From the East, for red is its color;
    From the North, for white is its color;
    From the West, for yellow is its color;
    And from the South, for blue is its color;
In the counterclockwise motion of *Tawa Taka*, the Sun Father,

Come the four colors of the races of humankind,
    each with its leaders,
    each with its destiny.
Soon they will fight, as it is prophesied,
but someday they shall unite.
    Then they will remember
    that Taiowa is their Spirit Father;
    that Sotuknang is their adoptive one;
    and that Spider Woman is the web
    which unites them all.

Through the power of this song, people of all races and color
were created. Through the power of the song, people will last,
if they remember to sing it in their heart.
Although they spoke different tongues at first,
       they were happy with each other.
There was no sickness, there was no evil, and they multiplied.

But then, first it was the animals who walked away.
Then also the enjoyment and the beauty
       of the world around them,
and of their own bodies, distracted them from the reasons
for it to be, and for which they came.
They forgot the instructions given by Taiowa,
       to sing the Song of Creation.
The ones who remembered were chastised.
Sotuknang said to them: "Leave your possessions, your homes,
 and your fields. Do not look back." And not with words,
but through the opening at the top of their heads,
which was still open, he told them of the secret name
of a place for them to gather.
       It was a hill, an ant hill.

Sotuknang hit the ground four times with his walking stick.
"I brought people to stay with you for a while,"
he said to the gatekeeper of the ant world.
"Welcome," the ant answered. "Lolamai."
The remnants of the first people moved in with the ant people
to be safe when Sotkunang destroyed Tokpela,
       the first world, with fire.

TOKPA: *The Second World*

It took some time for Sotuknang to find the right moment,
and the right place, and the right mood,
    to overcome his disappointment.
But he finally gathered enough strength to create a new world.
After his work was done, he went to tell the survivors
of the first world the time had come to come out.
"Great!" said the ant at the entrance. "Food is running short,
and our waists are getting smaller, and smaller."

"Before you emerge in this brand new world,"
Sotuknang said to his people,
    "Remember the pledge you made to Taiowa:
not to be greedy; to respect your neighbor and yourself,
and the spirit and body of woman, which is the body of
      Kokyang-Whuti, Spider Woman."

They all agreed.
The second world felt good to the people
after staying so long in the ant world. It was green and lush
everywhere; plants, flowers, even the grass, were gigantic.
Even the animals, strange animals they never saw before!
Much, much bigger than the ones of the first world.
So big in fact, that Sotuknang warned to stay away from them,
because they were mean, untamed, and ferocious.
So the people went in different directions, to build villages
in places best to grow their crops. They were happy
      as they sang the Song of Creation.

But then — Some became greedy! — though life was plentiful.
Greed made them fight one another.
Fight for more possessions, fight for women.
The ones who remembered the Song were criticized.
So Taiowa said to Sotuknang, "Destroy this second world!
People have forgotten the instructions I gave them,
they have forgotten their pledge to live according
to the original plan of life." Knowing that some remembered,
and still sang the Song of Creation, Sotuknang said to them,
"Go and take refuge with your brothers, the ants,
    when I destroy this wicked world."

With the Twins helping, so it was.
The world froze solid from pole to pole, and in its imbalance,
    the world stopped spinning for a while.

KUZ-KURZA: The Third World

In this world, humankind grew and grew,
spreading everywhere. They built large cities, civilizations,
they even created strange objects, like boxes which flew
    through the air.
Some became so powerful, they waged war
on the others, annihilating them with their machines.
They tried to change the course of Taiowa's life plan,
breeding some of them with animals
    to make a race of slaves.

Sotuknang said to Spider Woman, "The way things are going,
we must not let them kill each other any further.
But how could we save the ones who still know the song?"
"Go and find an old ant hill, one that the ants have vacated
for some reason. Then cut a hollow reed from the nearest pond.
Seal yourselves in the underground cache.
When I build the next world, when I am finished,
    use the reed to emerge in the new world."

Then Sotkuknang destroyed the third world.
A great flood covered the Earth; it rained for a full moon.
From the power of the unleashed winds, waves as big as mountains
    leveled everything there was.

But the remnants of the third world,
the ones who remembered the Song, were cozy and safe
    with Spider Woman to watch over them.

MAS-KI: The Underworld

The Hopi esoteric teaching on the Underworld has a similar place to Heaven in Christian beliefs. The Underworld underlies the entire system of thought which Hopi understanding of life and of the human race is based upon. Several Hopi beliefs dealing with the Underworld point out its essential place in the entire Hopi belief system.

First of all, they believe that present-day humanity is the "Fourth World," the fourth experiment of humankind in the world following three unsuccessful ones. Each living experiment originated in the Underworld, which is the mother or matrix. Each of these cycles, or "worlds," began its cycle like a fetus in the mother's womb.

Secondly, the spirit of the departed goes to the Underworld, Mas-Ki, wearing the mask that a member of the Catsina society wore during his initiation. This illustrates the prime importance of the Catsina clan in Hopi thought. In the Hopi Way, dead people's spirits go to the Underworld first before coming back as clouds in the sky, which gives them the name, "cloud people." When buried in the right way, it is believed the cloud people will bring rain to fall on the fields, helping the plants to grow.

It is said that during the third human cycle or "world," the God of the Earth, Masau, was demoted by Taiowa, God of

Creation from whom he received his commission as care-taker of the third world, because of misbehavior. But Masau is a god, and therefore a spirit, and cannot die. So, he was relegated to the function of God of Death and the Underworld. When the fourth world came into being, he was given another chance and promoted again to the role of Earth caretaker, which he occupies today.

Hopi underground ceremonial chambers, *kivas*, are symbolically representative of the Underworld. In each kiva, a small hole in the ground located in the middle of the chamber is called *sipapuni*, or, for short, *sipapu*. It is the symbol of Hopi emergence into the four worlds of physical reality.

Geological evidence also indicates a succession of geological cycles or worlds, when earth masses drifted as the spinning of the earth moved the underground plates during polar shift phases. These geological theories support the possibility of human development similar to the Hopi vision of the evolution of humanity. Even the esoteric theories about Atlantis, Lemuria, and Mu bear similarities to the story of the Hopi.

Catsinas come from the Underworld, as do the newly born, and then the dead return there. This is how important the Underworld concept is for the Hopi. They are so grounded in Mother Earth that it is natural for their Nirvana to be underneath the earth crust in an Underworld offering the comfort of the womb. This is the womb they believe they have issued from, and in the Judeo-Christian world, there are caves, caverns and underground passages that are holy, where temples, churches, and cathedrals have been built.

2 TUWA-KATSKI:

The Emergence In The Present World

The Myth of Emergence

The Emergence

Food was getting dangerously low. "Let us see
if the waters receded, and if this brand new world is safe
for us to emerge into," said Spider Woman.
They pushed the hollow reed clear to the top of their world,
making a tiny hole, to see if any water came through! None did.
After hearing some thumping sounds, coming from above,
Spider Woman said, "We must send someone to see
  if other people live there already."

First they sent *Kisa, the hawk*, climbing through the reed,
but he never came back. Then they sent *Pavo Kaya*,
the swift swallow. He did not come back either.
"It must be a good world," said the people!
"Let us send *Mot Sini*, the mockingbird. He is cunning and smart.
He will tell us what is in the Upperworld.
They were right. Mot Sini did come back and said,
"It is a beautiful world up there, full of sun, full of flowers.
The thumping sounds we heard, it is *Massoua*,
  god and guardian of the Earth.
He was working in his corn patch, and I asked him,
'Can the people, the remnants of the third world
you destroyed by water come and live with you?'
He answered, 'If they pledge to live according to the life plan
originally given them by Taiowa; and if they remember to sing
the sacred Song of Creation, they can come and ask for permission
  to live in this beautiful world with me.' "

When Mot Sini, the mockingbird, said that,
the people let out a loud cry of joy
     and sang the Song of Creation, with reverence for life.

So one by one, they climbed through the hollow reed,
and went to ask permission to stay with Massoua.
"This Earth has been created for all living things,"
he said to them. "The animals, the plants, the birds,
     and humankind.
Also the clouds in the sky, the water, and the fishes.
But because you can talk and think, because you still have
an opening on top of your head when you are born which
enables you to communicate with Taiowa without words,
I am going to delegate some of my responsibilities to you.
I am going to leave the Earth and all living things on it
in your care. I appoint you guardians of this new world.
Take care of it, protect it from pollution. It is your home.
If you watch over it, it will feed you, clothe you,
and keep your children and grandchildren healthy and happy.
There will be hard times, when you will doubt.
But never lose faith that what I told you today
     is the truth."

Then it was the turn of Spider Woman to speak.
"Trust the Woman Spirit, which I represent.
It will guide you, give you succor and peace, like a mother does.
Your great grandchildren will know me by many names.
It's all the same. Whenever you need me, I'll be there,
to nurture, and protect you. So that there will be no conflict
between men and women, man's role will be
to take care of the outdoors, and women will rule indoors
the family home. Now, go, multiply and prosper.

Build houses, villages, and cultivate fields of corn,
of beans, and squash. Be happy."

They named their first village *Oraibi*.
Some say they called it *Walpi*, and some others *Shungopovi*,
depending to which clan they belong.
The Hopi tell many stories. They all say the same thing,
as they all come from the same original people created by Taiowa,
     long, long ago.
Although many have forgotten, many will remember.
And as Massoua asked them, they will do their best
     to care for this beautiful world.
And to be sure they do not forget, they wrote it on a rock.
They wrote the life plan of the Hopi, and it is called Prophecy Rock.
Anyone can see it near the present village of Oraibi.
It tells of a world, plagued by doubts and miseries,
     afflicted by illness.
A world called "Koyaansquatsi," "world out of balance."
Perhaps people will remember.
Perhaps they will not remember Taiowa's instructions.
But it is written . . .
     on the face of the rock.

TUWA-KATSI:
The Emergence In The Present World

The myth of emergence is common to many of the Native American tribes in one form or another. Expressed in all sorts of different ways, it describes the same event at the origin of each group. In the Judeo-Christian tradition, the creation of Adam from a bit of mud and Eve from Adam's rib, the mythical Eden, is no more and no less plausible than the Hopi vision of the Underworld and the myth of emergence as recounted in this book.

How *homo sapiens* entered into history is described by each human group in the way best understandable to them. This formidable event, the emergence of humankind in the present-day world, has understandably made such an impact on the Hopi historical memory that several geographical areas are thought to be the place of emergence. The Grand Canyon is believed to be the mythical place of the emergence from the Underworld. In a more symbolic way, in each Hopi kiva, the "sipapu," the little opening into the Earth in the center of the kiva, is the reminder of the original opening through which the ancestors came.

If it was not for its cataclysmic character, the Hopi esoteric recollection of the event is put in such poetic and romantic terms that it could make the most wonderful children's story, ever reminding us all what both the Earth and its inhabitants went through during the process of evolution.

3 THE MIGRATIONS

Migration Symbol

THE MIGRATIONS

From the steaming jungles, where the powerful Maya stood,
where mighty pyramids watched over the people;
from the land of many trees, where Palatk-Wapi,
mysterious Red City of the South, once harbored some who today
call themselves the Hopi, the Twins watched over
    the destiny of the Quiche nation.

From the heights of the majestic Andes, Palatk-Wapi also
could have been hidden at the bottom of the most precipitous
gorge, Vilacabamba. Or could it have been Machu-Picchu,
sacred city of the Incas, from where they could have come,
    these children of the sun?

Eototo and *Aholi*, chief Catsinas, protectors of the Hopi people,
could you have come from the mysterious South? From land
or sea, you could have come. No one will ever know, unless
through the open door at the top of the head. Yes, the people
know, but they cannot tell. Buried among the sacred
memories, the teachings, and the myths, lies a knowledge of
the sea, and visions of the frozen heights. The aquiline profile
of some, the way their eyes squint when they look at the sun,
as in awe in front of *Viracocha*, Sun God of the Incas.
Someone could tell that they also are children of the sun.

What about the big cities they left behind?
Chaco, Aztec, Chimney Rock, Hovenweep?
Where did they learn the skills, the engineering, the stone cutting?
From their towns, paths go to the sea, paths go to the jungles.
The macaw, a sacred bird along with the turkey.
Ball playing was like in the South. Not as serious perhaps,
        so as to bring death to the loser,
but if not deadly, serious enough, nevertheless.
They wore shells like on the seashore.
Pueblo Bonito, Chettro Ketl, Rinconada. Anasazi sacred kivas,
sacred shrines, where migrations from the South,
and migrations from the North met.
On vast spaces of Mesoamerica, following their instructions,
the clans drew gigantic crosses, giant swastikas.
Leaving their footprints on many paths, to someday end
on the sand wastes of Hopi land —
        where they are today.

From the North, they left Hovenweep, Mesa Verde, Aztec.
Parrots, eagles, bows, sun, and tobacco, their symbols
were written on the walls of their ancient homes,
or on the stones along the path.
        They left the word.
The instructions of Taiowa had been followed.
Like at the center of the rattle Catsinas use,
the swastika gave the word. They kept theirs.
Walpi, Oraibi, Shumopovi, Shipaulovi, Hotevilla, Bakavi —
all bear witness. Migrations are fact, not fancy.
For the people of today, the migrations are the testimony
of the past, which has found its center at last,
of a universe which found its axis; the key of it all:
        Hopi Land!

THE MIGRATIONS

A lot has been written and said about the Hopi migrations, but little is known. The problem is to distinguish between Hopi mythology and Hopi history. Hundreds, if not thousands, of ancestral Hopi villages, abandoned during the course of their migrations, can be found as far north as Utah, as far east as Kansas, even as far south as South America. The fine line separating legend and history is shrouded in mystery. Studying the accounts of the migrations, one can easily get lost without the sixth sense of intuition to reconstruct what this important and unique feature of Hopi past is about.

In order to carry out a meditation on this essential portion of the Hopi spiritual dimension, I established a synthesis of all the migration patterns to bring out the spirit that motivated them. Their purpose was to find the promised Hopi land on which they now live. Each clan found its way to the motherland, and this is proof enough that they were connected spiritually. The clans accomplished this incredible journey even though they never physically met. It was the spirit from which they each received the instructions, from Taiowa the Creator, as handed to them by Massoua, the Earth god. There are so many clans: Snake, Sand, Horn, Bear, Pumpkin, Catsina, Badger, Sun, Mustard, Tobacco, Bow,

Bluebird . . .etc. It is the accomplishment of the journey which causes the Hopi, ultimately, to trust the spirit.

That the migrations of the clans are given so much emphasis in Hopi theology indicates their importance in Hopi thought and points out that the Hopi of today are, in fact, the descendants of those who participated in the migrations.

These groups traveled in prescribed patterns, according to instructions received individually for each group through the opening on top of the head, the *fontanelle*, which, according to Hopi legend, was still open at the time. Meditation, prayer, visions, prophecies, and oracles must also have contributed in keeping communications open between groups. According to today's Hopi, some clans could have come from the Pacific Coast, from a large portion of the Rockies, even from Canada. Graphic symbology pertaining to the migrations points out that they were completed following a cross and swastika pattern.

4 THE CEREMONIES

WUWUCHIM:
The First Phase of Creation

Without the revolving door of time, opening on
    the immensity of life,
nothing could celebrate the open door of life.
When the sun is ready to make its appearance each morning,
the first glow is a promise of a door which will open
on a new day. This solid mass, the Earth, once was a promise
for the future which does not cease to be.
The irridescent glow of spouting volcanoes, the tremors
of an unsettled land, offering the Earth's will to be.
The waters not yet born, the fire, this element
    of all beginnings, this is *Wuwuchim*,
a promise to germinate, manifesting itself through time.
Indeed it is the door leading to this stage of life on Earth.

New Fire Ceremony

New life, new fire.
Before the Catsinas ever come, there must be warmth,
     there must be life here on Earth.
Eototo says: "But there always was life in the particles of sand.
There was life — amoeba, lichen, protozoa — there was life,
     but no fire before this new day came to be.
There is no sun, so there is no fire!
But only the promise, Tawa, the Sun Father, will never fail to
warm the Earth. The transcendance of its prismatic power,
glowing from the shades of its irridescent colors,
     brings everything to life.

In the Hopi kivas, the new fire brings life for a new year,
perhaps for a new era, as prophecies have said!
The rite of life, the rite of hope. This is the same ritual
which makes the stars stay where they are, the sun shine,
     and the moon glow.
The ritual without which none of us would be here to talk about it,
and to keep on doing what Taiowa wants us to do:
Unite Tawa, the Sun Father, and Tuwa Katsi, the Earth Mother,
     in a Song of Creation.
For as long as we stay on this cradle, this arbor,
prepared for us to make use of, we will follow the sacred
writings on the rocks as they remind us to do.

Union of Tawa and Tuwa Katsi

The Rabbit Hunt

The men in a great circle, their rabbit sticks raised in
expectation, are handed *Somivikis* by the virgins
    in their sacred clothes.
So the rabbit hunt is held to honor Tawa, the Sun Father.
But still the Earth, this hot mass of gasses, pristine and radiant,
    has not yet cooled.
To permit the new day to come in
the memories of men and women, this new fire brings
the thought that once, before we were, the fire was.
As a reminder from all this: from the hills, the maidens,
the virgins, have come to bring us the ceremony of the new fire.
It will help us not to forget that once there was on Earth,
    nothing but fire.

The narrow alleys of Hopi are still dark,
waiting in the cold morn, waiting for the line of priests
to pass by for their ceremonial rounds.
Spider Woman's daughters keep the bowls of cold water
ready to cool the earth. Hot! From its germinating power,
they drench these men of learning, so they
    help the Earth to cool.

No one must come now; roads are closed,
no one dares to pass.
Initiates alone may see from the rooftops, the play,
to be the first for the year, opening the way for Catsinas
to return. So the men of the village dance in expectation,
in prayer and meditation. So the spirit fathers
find their way to the villages, the homes, and the people,
for a new day, a new year,
    a new life to begin.

Soyal

The Earth has cooled. From the East comes the golden glow,
forerunner of Tawa, the Sun Father. This is the second phase
of creation, the second day, second chance, second world.
Not cool enough for human, yet, but it welcomes the spirits of
things, of animals, of men — Catsinas. Along with the forests,
the animals, the mountains, green is everywhere.
    But still man must wait to enter.

This is Soyal, the blue-masked Catsina.
With a fiery red antenna, it opens the way to greet all that grows.
Hopis do not forget the germination process.
Soyal consecrates what Wuwuchim dedicated. Still half asleep
from its long rest since Niman, Soyal Catsina walks like a dream.
Walking like a dream blessing the Earth,
as it goes from village to village, street to street, door to door.
It opens the way for more, and more Catsinas,
to climb the steep trails made eons ago by Eototo and Aholi,
when they came from the mysterious Red City of the South,
    Palatk Wapi.

Matsop, the fertility Catsina, is here to make everything grow.
"Right on my tracks!" Soyal says. "But do not mind him,
his black mask with the white hands must not scare the women of
the Hopi. Do not fear his ways, for they are sacred ways
to keep life going. His way is dedication through fornication.
Matsop Catsina brings life, as Taiowa intended.
Not as a sin, but as a rite. The rite of life, rite of hope,
is the same ritual which makes the stars stay where they are,
    the sun shine and the moon glow.

This is the ritual without which none of us would be here
to talk about it and to keep on doing what Taiowa
wants us to do: Unite Tawa, the Sun Father, and Tuwa Katsi,
        the Earth Mother, in a Song of Creation.
For as long as we stay on this cradle, this arbor, which is
prepared for us to make use of, we will follow the sacred writings
on the rocks as they remind us to do." And in all the kivas,
the golden disk, image of the sun, dancing in front of sipapuni,
reminds us that without its power, its heat and light,
        earth would be barren.
And barren would women be,
        without Matsop and *Kokopelli.*

The Kiva Night Dances

They stomp on top of the kivas, asking for permission
to come and bring the people heavenly blessings.
Following Soyal and Matsop, the Catsinas have come
        in great numbers.

"Come in . . .come in . . ." says the kiva priest. "Bring joy and
health to the people! Come to regenerate the Earth, procreate
and germinate the corn, the soil, the waters, and our women."

In great numbers they come.
Through the sipapuni at the top of the kiva, they enter
the Underworld, where all things come to and return to.
Long-Hair Catsinas, Supai, Mixed Catsinas and Navajos,
Hililis, Heheyas and Koyemsis — all the Catsinas
bring to the people, deep in fervent attention,
the blessings of the gods, for they are the messengers.
The phantasmagoric display of the godly dimensions
        here on earth is over.

Pamuya, this moon in which Soyal came to be, give room to
Powamuya, the last phase of the myths of Creation.

Koyemsis Going to the Kiva

POWAMU: *The Last Myth of Creation*

What Wuwuchim planned in a world in formation,
Soyal codified as the Earth solidified herself.
Now Powamu will sanctify it, bringing on the world scene
after plants, and the animals, humankind,
     jewel of creation.
Taiowa himself saw fit to bring this conscious witness of the
great mystery play, with no time limit, no boundaries, but also
no guarantees. For it keeps on repeating itself within cycles
and surges of energy, bountiful and limitless.

Humankind's responsibility is enormous.
Such a beautiful world, "Lolamai!"
The confidence placed on humankind's shoulders, the trust
of its wisdom and abilities, makes it the experiment
that might have no duplication anywhere. And no precedent either!
Therefore there is no means of comparison
     in the whole universal plan.
This is why Taiowa said: "Keep on singing the Song of Creation.
It will keep you from sinning, to the depths of oblivion."

Powamu is confirmation of the Song,
     an affirmation and assurance.
Stones are being quarried, sand is being brought,
and the home will be built as the site has been chosen,
and the foundations are being laid! The architect drew the plan;
now, final execution is up to the people.
If they spare their strength, amplify their wisdom,
and cultivate their foresight, they will be guided in the dark days,
     through the blessings of the gods.

Taiowa is the breath, humankind is the mouthpiece,
to carry the sounds of creation to the far reaches of eternity.
The people are the building material, bringing on their wings
  the lessons of time.
Timelessness, selflessness, oneness are rhythms of
  the song the Hopi know well!

Powamu starts in the kivas with the planting of the beans,
and with a song to mother nature she knows well,
and has repeated year after year since the Earth cooled.
With the breath of faith and the warmth of the sipapuni,
the sprouts grow fast in the warmth of the kivas.
The people receive the bundled sprouts in reverence,
a gift they all share as brothers and sisters.
A sign of many blessings and community of souls,
with faith in the destiny of the people, together singing
  the song that keeps life on the path of creation.

Initiation

For the song to be sung,
words must be taught to boys and girls, the people of tomorrow.
 At the end of the long day, ceremonial fathers and mothers
lead the way to the kiva, where secrets
are finally revealed, and flesh slightly wounded
    by the yucca whips of *Tungwup* and his Catcinas.

As seen by Crow Mother, the teachings of life
and its responsibilities are taught,
along with the strength of the warrior's way.
"No. . .no," the parents say, "the children are good."
"No. . .no," the priest says, "Whip me first." "We are the teachers,"
the Catsina reply, "the spirit fathers and Taiowa's helpers.
Without strength the children will die. Trust us.
We know what is best for them, for in the end. . .all is well,
as it is not the end, but a beginning, for a life filled with
responsibilities, and joy, and gifts, and exchanges,
and love under a different name!
    Lolamai is the name."

The Great Sipapuni Initiation

The Bean Dance

Sacred bean sprouts, blessed in the kiva, and shared by all.
The sacrament of communion is observed.
Hopis gather in closeness and unity in the night,
to pray and to share the intimate space of the kiva.
This is the Hopi Way, brotherhood and sisterhood,
in the warmth of the common womb.
The mystery play is about to begin, *Palulukang*,
    the water serpent, appears.
Guardian spirit of Powamu; the sacred Twins; Aholi, Eototo,
and Crow Mother — all protectors of the people —
    watch with great vigilance.
For Catsinas will appear unmasked this time.

Soyoko

Below the mesa, there is noise and commotion;
children run in all directions seeking shelter in friendly houses.
A long procession of monster Catsinas who serve as bodyguards,
protecting *Soyok Wuhti*, the Black Ogre Woman, appears.
She wants food, lest she roast the children who
misbehaved during the year. Saws dragging on the ground
make an awful raspy sound. Clicks of the swords,
mixed with cries and shouts, fill the air.
Here come *Soyok*, *Taka*, *Nataska*, *Tahrum* and *Wiharu*,
the White Ogre, surrounding the awful figure of Soyok Wuhti,
        the ogre woman.
Her red tongue is hanging out from a toothless mouth.
She has straggling hair, and staring eyes,
and carries a blood-smeared knife and a long white jangling crook
        to catch naughty children.
She is truly a fearsome figure, shouting,
"Hoo-hoo! Hoo-hoo!" from one end of the village
        to the other.
"My children have been good,
" pleads the mother. "We want meat," is the answer.
"What about this pot of stew?" That is the compromise,
        so Soyok Wuhti can move on.

The Soyoko ritual is the closing of Powamu,
the end of the three-part play of the Hopi Way,
which relives the drama of the Creation, which Wuwuchim
inaugurates in the greyish glow of the first phase.

Then Soyal solidified the earth with the appearance of the
first Catsinas. As the horizon grew more yellow with Powamu,
humankind is initiated at last, with the red sunrise,
the herald of the glorious globe of the rising sun.

It is *Talawa*, the new dawn Catsina at last.

THE NIMAN CATSINA:
The Going-Home Ceremony

Spirit of the Eagle, spirit of the morning star;
spirit of Massoua, spirit of the ancients;
the ants and all the animals — the ones the Hopi call Catsinas
— since winter solstice and the new fire ceremony,
you extend your protection through your presence
    on the Hopi mesas.
But now the time has come for you to go on the other
side of the world, where people and crops need the warmth
of your rays. Ever since you blessed us through Wuwuchim,
in the Upperworld, we enjoyed your presence.
Now you are needed in the Underworld for a while.

Hemis Catcinas

The San Francisco Peaks will be your sipapuni,
through which your path will be granted.
So go with the people's blessing and the sacrifices of the Eagle,
messenger of the Hopi, Kwahu, our brother Eagle.

In the early spring when the Sun Father shared with us
his softest rays, when his warmth was needed
for new burgeoning, then the time was for the clans
        to gather the eaglets.
Quite unaware then of the great honor besetting them,
the little bundles of yellow feathers were carefully selected
to become our Hopi brothers and messengers,
like Catsinas, to carry the messages of the people
        to the Creator, the great equalizer of all things.

Gathering of the Spruce

Symbolizing life itself, sharing their vitality and their grace,
the green limbs are gathered, and brought to the villages,
    bringing strength, life, and permanence.
Kaibab, the great forest of the north, Grand Canyon,
sipapuni of the West, San Francisco Peaks, mountain of the south—
all holding the sacred spruce for Hopi to gather.
And Catsinas provide spruce for farmers,
placing it in the middle of their fields.
After the blessings of the ceremony, a prayer is said
for growth, plenty and fruition, for Catsinas and the Earth,
    and for the Sun.
This is a winning combination which brings assurance
    of germination.

The Dance

Mysterious, secretive, and foreboding,
midnight brings the sounds of the ritual that no one is about to see.
Only the ears as witness capture the song of the Catsinas.
On the deserted village square, coming from the kivas,
they dance, watched by the moon, and surrounded by
     the deep silence of the night.

The magenta glow of the rising sun
brings Talawa, the sunrise Catsina, for an early blessing.
The magnificence of the Hemis catsinas fill the *Kisonvi*,
the sacred center of the village, along with myriads
of great bundles of early sweet corn plants,
covering the center square, several feet high.
     The moment is awesome.

Then the great blessing starts. All the people begin the
long line that will move from one Catsina to the other,
puffing the sacred corn meal on each one of the sacred beings'
shoulders. After blessing it with their breath,
blessing the sacred shrine of the village:
"*Bonsai!*" says the priest.
"Ugh . . . gh . . . gh . . ." reply the Catsinas.
Undulating and uncoiling, the long line, its song in motion,
starts moving with the motions of a huge snake,
     like the waves of the sea.

The sounds of the rattles, the turtle shells, and the bells —
a hypnotic chant,
from somber tones slipping through the masks,
uniting all the Hopi, visitors, bystanders — through the
power of this meditation, along with the rest of the world.
Catsina dolls for little girls, bows and arrows for boys,
plaques, baskets, *piki*, fruits and vegetables for those who
deserve the messengers' attention. It all comes so fast,
till Tawa, the Sun Father,
starts to sink in the other side of the Earth.

The final glow of the powerful prayers ends with priests and
priestesses collecting *pahos*, spruce and feathers
that gods and messengers made sacred.
    All fades at the end of the day,
leaving behind the accomplishments of well-spent rituals,
    bringing love, health, and "giveaway."

The Sacrifice of the Eagles

Most powerful of all is the sending of Kwahu to the heavens,
to reaches never attainable with his wings alone.
Loaded with gifts, festooned with prayers,
he leaves behind his feathers to his earthly brothers and sisters,
to remember the power of his strokes. So they imitate,
in due time and in proper places, the flight of the eagle,
king of the birds, as he reaches the highest clouds.
He sends, from the silence above, his unique cry,
that only trained ears and heart will ever be able to capture
and understand.

The Hopi Man-Eagle

THE CEREMONIES

Ceremonies are the channel, the pipeline through which the very soul of a people flows through the ages. Without a ceremonial life, the essence of a civilization or a society will not stand the test of time. Ceremonies can follow the same ritual repeatedly, but they also evolve, as the people move toward new horizons. In fact, such changes should be considered healthy, for they reflect that human cycles are not stagnant but are constantly evolving. Ceremonies will help the process, as they insure protection, security, balance, and coordination, easing the way and preventing chaos or psychological breakdown that could destroy balance and the goals of evolution. In Hopi terms, this means following the instructions given originally by Taiowa, the Creator — a plan that perhaps seems obscure unless seen through the spirit which gives it its sense and vitality. A partial vision of the plan over time could trigger a philosophy of despair and hopelessness.

So many times, the human race felt neglected, even forsaken, instead of reinforcing its will to survive against all odds. Taiowa, the Creator, is there if mankind is willing to listen. As the Hopi put it, "Sing the Song of Creation," which ensures the continuum. This is what the Hopi ceremonies are about: celebrating time after time the deep mystery of creation, staging for the faithful an annual set of mystery plays, underlying the creation plan so it does not get lost in the shuffle of everyday living.

The Hopi prophecies, some of which are inscribed on the rock at Oraibi, are a master plan given by Taiowa, to be enforced by Massoua, the Earth guardian, by Sotuknang, his helper and nephew, and Spider Woman, archetype of the Great Mother, without which no creation could take place. From time to time, the web wears out and needs repairs, and this is what gives struggling humanity the feeling of neglect, leading to depression and despair. The ceremony becomes paramount, as it reminds the people along the way that if the ground seems unsteady, this is no time to grow insecure. Patience and faith, singing the Song of Creation, this is what the ceremonies are about. This will pull the people through the specific realities of the plan. In spite of outside pressures put on them by the successive invaders into their secret world, the ceremonies are today what they always have been, the expression of the very soul of the Hopi people.

Life must be paid with life, ancient America tells us. The earth must periodically die to ensure its rebirth. This is a catastrophic vision of evolution, a cyclic pattern of creation which is supported by modern science. Ceremonial life helps the Hopi go from transition to transition, from stone to stone, as they cross the torrent of life. This yearly succession of Hopi ceremonies projects a feeling of stability that many people in the industrial and technological world would find beneficial as their own structures become unbalanced under the pressure of rapid changes.

It is impossible to present Hopi ceremonies in a simplistic manner, and it is not the purpose of this book to do so. But the structure of the Hopi calendar, which is divided into four major events, will help the reader to identify with the yearly unfolding and enter into the Hopi dimension. The reader must keep in mind that all Hopi rituals come from great amounts of time, meditation, and concentration in the kivas. Because the purpose of Hopi ceremonies is to rejoin with the rest of the world, Caucasians and other Native Americans are welcome when the ceremony takes place in the village streets or the central square, and even when certain ceremonies are held in the kivas. In the Bean Dance, in early spring, the public unknowingly symbolizes the world at large, an essential part of the ceremony itself.

An essential element of Hopi ceremonial life is also the making and use of pahos. Pahos are sacramental objects, usually blessed ceremonially in the kiva, consisting of a down feather from an eagle or wild turkey, attached to a string of native cotton. Pahos hold a lot of power, as they symbolize the "thread" that exists between people and the Great Spirit. No Hopi ceremonial activity is held without the making and use of pahos, which will be placed later at sacred places in the home, in the kivas, or at the numerous shrines and sacred springs all over the Hopi land.

Another element of Hopi sacramental activity is corn meal. It is intended to be a meal for supernatural beings only. Corn meal is used in every facet of ceremonial life at Hopi—to open or close the paths that lead to spiritual involvement, to bless the Catsinas, people, and places. It is a cleansing and nurturing process; it symbolizes the fertilization of the cere-monies, the blessing of the string of people, and places. Corn meal can be made from white or blue corn, and it is ground ceremonially on a grinding stone to a fine meal to be stored in a small pouch. It is spread easily by the person doing a blessing with three fingers.

Piki bread is a paper-thin roll made of blue corn meal and ashes. It is used in lavish quantities in the social gatherings which occur around the ceremonies, and it is a form of sacramental communion. Somiviki is identical to a Mexican tamale, made of cooked blue corn meal, and indicates that the Mexicans adapted the Indian specialty to their taste. Pikami is a pudding made from wheat and corn sprouts, baked in a hole dug in the ground.

All three forms of ceremonial meal are pure Hopi, not influenced by outside cultures. The meal is used lavishly in many ceremonies. The making, use, and consumption will be described in detail in the next chapter, "The Hopi Social Cycle." They indeed are analogous to the bread and wine of the sacrament of Communion.

Kivas, pahos, and corn meal are the substances from which spring Hopi ceremonies, and interwoven are the shrines, creating a web of religious fervor that ignites the very life of the ceremonies themselves. The two main societies controling the ceremonial calendar are the *Catsinup* and Powamu. Every Hopi child must be initiated in either one of them. And the four main ceremonial cycles of Hopi life are Wuwuchim, Soyal, Powamu and Niman.

WUWUCHIM: *The First Phase of Creation*

The Hopi ceremonial year begins with the first phase of a three-phase cycle to celebrate the whole process of creation. This first aspect is called Wuwuchim. "Wu" means to germinate, and "Chim," to manifest. Depending on the village, this celebration will take place some time in November. In Hopi spirituality, everything, every object, has two aspects, the material and the supernatural. This characterizes the two halves of the Hopi universe, based on the path of the sun in the visible world during the daytime and the invisible one during the hours of the night. After sunset, Tawa, the Sun Father, is thought to begin the journey in the Underworld until he is reborn again at the start of a new day. This calls for a daily celebration and blessing as each new day dawns.

Interaction between the two halves of the Hopi world is established by the Catsina rituals, or Catsinup, the use of pahos and corn meal, and ritual smoking, in or out of the kivas. This is offered to the Catsinas, for they are representatives of the supernatural realm and its deities under the leadership of Taiowa, the Creator. In Hopi thinking, as the supernatural forces are being petitioned, they must reciprocate by giving things in return, such as rain, proper weather conditions, or other benefits that will promote fertility. This process of barter is at the base of everyday Hopi life and is a very basic form of sympathetic magic.

The three ceremonial events — Wuwuchim, Soyal, and Powamu — trigger the whole process of creation in plants, animals and humankind. The ceremony of Wuwuchim opens with "The New Fire Ceremony." It is held at dawn just before the sun appears on the horizon, and the red coals of this ceremonial fire will serve to light the fires in all the kivas. It will end by a truly collective baptism of the new ceremonial year, when the women of the village ritually douse the men involved in the ceremony with buckets of cold water, regardless of the coolness of the November day.

The creative fire is now lit, the emergence is reenacted, and man's evolutionary cycle is initiated.

SOYAL: *New Life*

Soyal ("so" meaning all, "yal" meaning year) is held during the month of December, and is the second great ceremony of the year. It opens the door for the Catsinas' return from the San Francisco Peaks. No public dance is held; it is a period of silence, concentration, and fasting. It is held primarily in the kivas, the kiva being the doorway between the supernatural world (the Underworld) and the normal everyday field of experience. The time of Soyal is determined by solar observations, telling the men in the kivas to prepare the pahos that will be deposited at the shrines after the ritual smoking over them has empowered them to send the prayers of the people to the power spirits.

Soyal corresponds to winter solstice, "The Return of the Sun," as the Hopi call it, which has been slipping away as daylight became shorter. For each village, the purpose of the ritual is to "open" the kivas for the Catsinas' return.

The ceremony begins with the appearance of a single Catsina, the Soyal, displaying a radiant blue mask surmounted by a fiery bright red spike, symbolizing the rising sun. It is the first Catsina to appear on the mesas, walking with an uncertain pace as if coming out of a deep sleep, which the Hopi believe has lasted since the Catsinas left for the underworld at the last home dance in July, Niman.

Then a second Catsina appears, a frightening figure all in black with white hands painted on its mask and body. It is the Matsop Catsina, portraying the male fertility power, and it symbolizes procreation. It goes around the villages simulating copulation, but only with married women and not with virgin girls. Women often volunteer to participate in the ceremony, especially ones who have lost an infant, hoping in this way of symbolic magic to have another child to take the place of the departed one.

Dominated by silence, solemnity, and secrecy, the Soyal celebration goes on in the kivas as Tawa, the Sun Father, is being venerated on his return to the Earth after his stay in the

Underworld since the last Niman ceremony the previous July.

During the Soyal ceremony, a young maiden, called the Hawk Maiden, always from the Parrot clan, will sit in the kiva on a plaque or flat dish like a basket on which pahos and all sorts of seeds have been deposited. This signifies the female function of reproduction. Then ends this very important ceremony, which signifies that life has been "germinated," celebrating the second phase of creation, or second world.

In the following *Pamuya* month, the path that has been opened by the Soyal Catsina will be followed by hundreds of Catsinas, who will appear in the kivas in a cycle called Catsina Night Dances. They herald the third phase of this mystery play of related rites promoting fertility and germination. The last phase of the process of creation is called "Powamu."

POWAMU: *The Purification*

Powamuya symbolizes the last phase of creation. Wuwuchim laid the pattern of life for the coming year, Soyal agreed to it, and Powamu purifies it. In its eight days of preparation and eight days of rituals, it portrays life in its full physical form.

The Powamu ceremonial cycle is divided into the planting of the beans in the kivas, the children's initiations, and the appearance of Soyoko. Beans will germinate under forced heat before the ceremony is over, using the power of sympathetic magic to influence nature. At the time of the Bean Dance, the long bean sprouts will be cut, tied in bundles, and distributed in the village. Every household will cook them with their stew in a beautiful and simple form of the communion ritual.

The initiation of Hopi children takes place between the ages of six and ten. They have to be initiated at that time in either the Catsina or the Powamu societies. Led by their ceremonial fathers, they will be presented to the whipping Catsinas in a pure state of nakedness to be ceremonially whipped, and it is then that they will learn that Catsinas are impersonated by men of the village, often their relatives. Long ago, it is said, Catsinas could be seen by the Hopi in their spirit form, but it is also said that today the people have lost this ability.

The Bean Dance then follows in the kivas, with Aholi and Eototo, the two chief Catsinas who once came from the mysterious city of the south called Palatkwapi. They are accompanied by Crow Mother Catsina. The Catsinas taking part in the dance are unmasked, so all children present must have been initiated prior to the ceremony and given full knowledge of the meaning of the Powamu ceremony, which will help them carry out their duties as initiated members of Hopi society.

Finally, a gruesome chapter of the ceremony will take place when Soyoko, the black ogress, appears on the mesa with her entourage of awesome monsters and ogres to scare children (and sometimes outsiders) out of their wits. The frightening group go from house to house demanding food or they will take the children and roast them. It is quite a sight to see parents argue with the black Catsina to prove to her, by giving her good stew or pies or cookies, that their children have behaved right all along. It is an efficient way to maintain parental authority and remind youngsters of their future responsibilities as members of Hopi society.

The reenactment of the three phases of creation are now completed. Wuwuchim, Soyal, and Powamu are the corner-stones of Hopi ceremonialism as they synchronize the path of the sun and of humankind together.

THE NIMAN CATSINA CEREMONY:
Going-Home Ceremony

Closing the entire cycle is the Niman or Catsina Going—Home Ceremony. It takes place toward the end of July or the first week in August, depending on the village. Considered to be a summer solstice celebration, Niman coincides with the beginning of harvest of the early sweet corn. Huge bundles of corn are carried by the Niman Catsinas as they make their appearance in the kisonvi, the village square, at sunrise. The feeling is overwhelming, as more than thirty of the tall, masked beings enter the plaza as the sun makes its appearance. The village square is filled with high bundles of early corn and stalks, with Catsina dolls attached for the girls and bows and arrows for the boys. It indeed celebrates life, as the sun warms the abundance. Niman truly is the harvesting of the winter prayers brought about during Soyal and Powamu through the manifestation of the powerful force of germination, using heat, moisture, and air. The Niman ceremonial cycle ends with the Niman Catsina dance, held in the village main plaza. After the dance is over at sunset, the Catsinas leave for the San Francisco Peaks above Flagstaff, their spiritual home when not in the villages.

The whole Niman ceremonial cycle is divided into several phases. First, the eagles are gathered in the early spring, when eaglets are only a few weeks old. Each clan controls a certain number of nests, and eagles will be taken, leaving enough eaglets in the nest for the next generation. Secondly, the spruce is gathered, to be erected on the plaza and to be worn by the Catsinas around their waist. Evergreens symbolize life everlasting. The dance itself is most often performed by the Hemis Catsinas, awesome figures very popular among the villagers, who dance from sunrise to sunset. They are truly a magnificent display, reminiscent of the days when giants were on earth.

Finally, the cycle of the yearly Catsina ceremonial calendar ends with the sacrifice of the eagles, perhaps one of the most mysterious aspects of the whole ceremonial cycle. As the Christ sacrifice is an essential part of Christian liturgy and doctrine, so the eagle, true brother of the Hopi, is entrusted with the great honor of carrying the petitions and prayers of the people. Sacrificed without bloodshed, the soul of Kwahu, the eagle, is released to go to the land of the cloud people, rising in the firmament to rejoin Taiowa, the Creator. Eagle feathers are venerated and used in the ceremonies, and the body of the eagle is ceremoniously buried in a special cemetery, with all the pomp and solemnity of a human burial.

5 THE HOPI SOCIAL CYCLE

I: *The Cry*

The life that once came to the Hopi, is celebrated today,
and every day. Wuwuchim, Soyal, Powamu, Niman,
essence of all life comes still from the depths
    of the American desert.
High on the Hopi mesas, a babe, a child,
essence of the people, is born.
Symbol of what is Hopi, of its claim to life,
a guarantee of its message to the world
that the clans once brought long, long ago. Still it is today,
for a child is born at Hopi every day —
born of the people's faith, its confidence, and its energy.
For it is what makes Hopi. It will live, it will survive
    through its children.

When the day finally draws to a close, and night falls on the
mesas, when Tawa starts his trip to the other side,
the butterfly girls, anxious to try their wings,
    slip out of the houses.
And running, jumping even perhaps, over boulders,
and sliding on the sand hills with the strength and the speed
of youth, they are driven by the call of nature deep within
    to find the mate.

It is the child, pushing its way through to find a family,
    a channel, a stage, to play its part.
In the Hopi drama of life, it is the child who needs to manifest
its presence, and its right to have the chance to live.

Boys beware, as you hold the golden key with which
Taiowa, the creator, wants you to open the way
    for the new life to come;
so the Creator's will be done.
The music has been written, the song has been sung.
Now the new life out of the depth of the most celebrated
rite on Earth, comes the child.

No ritual, no human act, has more impact, bears more fruits,
more joy and sorrows than when the key which fits into the
lock, opens the sacred chest, to reveal its secrets.

In a grandmother's arms, shaded from Tawa's rays,
the new babe lays immersed in love and rabbit furs,
for the twentieth day has not arisen yet.

The tension mounts till the day when the Sun Father
will shower its warm rays on this new life
and consecrate its existence for years to come.
Water is being warmed, yucca roots ground.
The sacred suds will bathe the baby in delight.
A perfect white mother corn is chosen,
and when the face whitens with the sacred corn meal,
the child will be presented to the Sun Father at last.

The twentieth day at last,
underscores the first light of the eventful day.
Protected from the bite of the morning chill,
the slight baby is wrapped in the fur blanket by the grandmother,
who waits for the first ray to slip out of the horizon.
This first blinking speck of light of the heavenly body in motion,
    brings the blessing, the caress of light.

The baby's soul will capture this sacred moment
and keep it for a lifetime, as the most intimate
and the most vivid testimony of life.
It is the moment when Taiowa's spirit meets the baby's,
       when Creator meets Creation.
Blessed and refreshed, the new Hopi soul
now comes to the fold, in reverence
       and in communion.

Joining in the meditation with the grandmothers
and the grandfathers, departed long ago, aunts, uncles,
brothers and sisters, future mothers and sisters,
sit ceremoniously on the floor, around the ritual foods
that sustained the Hopi in generations past
       and in times to come.
Piki, pikami, somiviki have sustained Hopi bodies,
even the soul, so that the songs, the teachings
and the rites will pass along from generation to generation
through the children who lay motionless
       in their rabbit blankets.

II. The Motion

From the security of the blanket, the warmth of the house,
the love of the mother, the child now moves away
toward a new security — to the people!
It is now initiation. Godfathers and godmothers,
under the cover of darkness, bring the children
to the kivas, to the whipping Catsinas.
Many a cry, many a tear, from parents and children
    reflect the thorny path of life.
This first initiation, a guide, a protection, a lifeline.

This first mystery opens realities of life and mystical realities
of a vision quest, the truths of the Catsina world.
Now comes the real test: initiation into manhood,
initiation into womanhood. The mystical warrior to be,
and the Earth Mother, the clan mother,
    and the corn mother to be.

For a long time, Catsinas brought dolls to the little girls,
bow and arrows to the little boys, and baskets full of fruits
to the rest. But now time has come for the gifts to be given
by those children of yesterday —
    for they are the adults of tomorrow.

On her knees, the long hours passing by,
the young woman grinds, grinds, and grinds.
For this is the beginning of the initiation.
She is shaded from the sun, as the little babe she once was,
in the little piki house, full of silence, language of the gods.
    For four days she'll be talking to them.

In her meditation, grinding the sacred blue corn for piki
to be baked, for piki to be given,
this gift of the unspoken gods of the Hopi universe.
Purified, sanctified, the young woman —
    now priestess of her world —
will bring her long, black, lustrous hair
to be ceremonially washed in yucca suds on the 5th day.

As ore from deep in the mine must also be purified,
so too pure gold can be brought to the fore.

So humans must also be purified for Taiowa, gold to be.
So now the butterfly hairdo that adorns the Hopi maiden
will be her new wings to fly toward the woman to be,
    to the boy she loves.
when the last rays of the sun light the end of a day,
she'll run toward the place where the lovers meet,
    to practice being mothers and fathers.

Puberty rites, adolescence rituals, vision quests —
the boys will follow on their way to manhood.
Racing from shrine to shrine, from sacred spring
to sacred spring, the warrior will emerge!
Learning of the power and the making of the paho.
Sending the blue smoke from the clay pipe clear into the sky
through the opening of the kiva, where the ladder stands,
bridging the two worlds. He will learn the sacred path
that leads to the Underworld through the sipapuni.
The sacredness of life is kept in his heart,
for the boy is no more, the man is finally here.

≪ *Hopi Maiden*

III. The Seal

On the road of life, no step will ever be a more important one
for man and for woman than the Hopi wedding ceremony.
Butterfly maiden wings supported her, guided her,
to the flower, to the tree, where strength
mixed with honeybee, made the marriage that was needed to be.
Through this age-old ritual that makes all of us the group,
the people, the Hopi, we will live, grow in unison,
fulfilling Taiowa's mission.
She sings for all to hear, while raising the children.
 But above all, she sings the Song of Creation.

For months, from the house of the man to the house of
the woman, gifts have been received and acknowledged.
A dike, a bridge, a foundation, is raised as time goes on.
A new family, a new household — this major block of Hopi life
keeps on growing to assume its role.
For the peaceful ones, as the prophecies claim,
are the ones without which there is no balance.

For four days, on her knees, the bride will grind corn.
The aunts, mothers, and grandmothers will bake piki,
 mountains of piki.
She grinds corn so the family tree will pass on the teaching,
 so she can make Hopi continue to exist.

As the sacred suds clean and purify the bride and groom,
in gentleness, quiet, and peace, the washing of the hair
takes place. Elders, aunts, and children,
in reverence and in silence, listen to the old grandmother
give her advice to the bride, as she has done many times before.
    The moment is awesome.

Praying, heads bowed together, meditating and renewing
Hopi collective strength, the essence of their destiny and
purpose is the ceremony itself.

For all to see, displayed on the nearby bed
is the virginal white robe. This sacred garment the uncle wove
in meditation, peace and silence, in his kiva.
Now the dressing of the bride begins: the black manta;
the red and green sash of the Hopi; the white boots,
that once, deep in the forest, the mighty deer,
brother of the Hopi, gave his furry hide for.
Now tanned and pure, they are the symbol
    of the woman's steps,
imprinting themselves so lightly on Mother Earth.

Symbolic, private and sensual, the moment where
for the first time, adorning the bride's face,
the hairdo of the matron will distinguish her as the woman,
    the mother, and the bride to be.
Adding to the magic of the moment,
in reverent silence, fabric of Hopi time,
everyone hands her a piece of the symbolic clothing.
The bride dresses, piece by piece, moment by moment,
symbol of the whole of Hopi, that she is marrying, too.
The Hopi woman stands on the goddess within,
    in grace, strength, and majesty.

Accompanying the bride to be, in procession,
    is the whole family.
From her house to his, leaving the past behind,
they step forward with resolution.
Her footsteps now will lead her to a tomorrow full of life —
    of Hopi life.
In the distance are the laughs, the noises,
the clashes of the mud fight between the rest of the family,
the same way it has been honored for centuries.
A goddess for one day, she is adorned and holy.
This is her day, surrounded by Catsinas.
When the power of their song blesses the virginal apparition.
She stands silently, reverently, at the end of their dancing line,
her eyes fixed on Tuwa Katsi as an homage to the Earth Mother.
Her contribution, her gift, is her wedding —
    for the Hopi to survive and to live.

IV: *The Conclusion*

The heart now stopped, its wings folded like Kwahu,
the sacred eagle, in his sacrifice, the departed Hopi
stands alone now, to be readied for the trip to the Underworld,
    and ultimately to the cloud country.
But before it can be — that this new Catsina can bring strength,
    rain and health to Hopi:
that the soil can be tilled and children be raised
and moisture come — the Hopi must pray.
For the departed has one more duty to his people —
to be the messenger, the link, and the bridge between the
realm of the living and the land of the spirit.
For this is no death, but one more way to be Hopi. . .once more.

Now stilled, the desert dweller is washed, blessed,
and dressed. For one more instant, is among his relatives,
in the home he loved, lying on the earth he defended,
    his body will pass all of this day.
Now its longtime duty has stopped. After the four ritual days,
there is a new home for the Underworld-bound Hopi.
Religiously, reverently, the mask of wild cotton is made
that the cloud people will recognize him.
The blackened chin will tell them, too. A crown of pahos
is made for the long journey ahead, which is full of dangers,
full of blocks and detours, for it is a hero's journey.
The soul might be hungry on the way; piki, meat,
and dried peaches will sweeten the fray.
With love, perhaps regrets, this
    Hopi will now be on his way.

Below the village, the sand hill lies in the sun.
Leslie, Alta, Patsy — and so many others rest there,
under the warm sand, close to home, close to Hopi.
The desert in its immensity lies at their feet, wild flowers
growing aplenty on this oasis below the rocky mesa.
Hopi, their land, their life, is all there, for everyone to see.
Inert and protective, the heavy white stones lay atop
only until their bone structures stay. No matter!
For the planting stick offers the energy to reach the heavens,
for it is painted blue. It is a symbol of another
ladder from the Underworld to the Upperworld —
the same ladder that once went from the first, the second,
and the third world into this one. . .our world.
The Hopi that lies under the warm sand of Toreva's hill,
next to the sacred spring of initiation, knows now he reached
the end of his journey, forever singing
    Taiowa's Song of Creation.

THE HOPI SOCIAL CYCLE

In no other place are social contacts and obligations so deeply rooted in spirituality and rituals as they are at Hopi. It is right to say that the energy that goes from one person to another at Hopi is balanced by as much spiritual input and religious fervor as the biological motion itself.

First, birth and the name-giving ceremony starts the cycle. Second are the initiations of children and young adults of both sexes. Next is the marriage ceremony, one of the most important moments in Hopi social life. Every Hopi issues from the mother principle, and the marriage ceremony portrays the spiritual marriage. The more solid the marriage, the more effective both the individual and the group will be. This ceremony is the basis of any clan society. The last rituals have to do with death and the departure to the underworld and the land of the cloud people. These are the main ceremonies that ritualize the four main events that divide the Hopi calendar.

The Hopi view the human life cycle as a pilgrimage from birth to death. Childhood, youth, adulthood, and old age succeed one another, and because of their transitory character, the way of the Hopi is to celebrate each passage. The ultimate experience that closes the road of life is death and the rebirth in the Underworld. This closes the cycle that began when the child was presented to Tawa, the Sun Father, on its twentieth day of life.

NAME-GIVING CEREMONY

The first ceremonial event marking the arrival of a Hopi child is the "Giving of the Name Ceremony." The equivalent of baptism in Christian society, it is the first ritual of the new life. The new arrival already has a function as far as the group is concerned, which is to renew the group life force. This is why children are so important in Hopi tribal structure from the very day of their birth. The advent of children in Western society is generally celebrated on a parental or a family basis, rather than seeing it as the glorification of the survival of the group. For a small group such as the Hopi, it takes an entirely different perspective. Children are their survival force.

After a child's birth, on its twentieth day, its hair is ceremonially washed as a symbol of purification. Its little face is ceremonially cleansed with sacred corn meal, which will be done again at the end of life in preparation for the journey to the Underworld. The paternal grandmother then blesses the child by gently rubbing its body with a perfect ear of white corn, called a "mother corn." Then as the rising sun begins to make its appearance for a new day, the child is presented to Tawa for the first time, wrapped in its best blanket, so that the sun's first rays touch the child's face, blessing it. Every detail of this gift of life is celebrated, making it a continual feast.

The simple and intimate ceremony of the name-giving finally concludes with a family feast in which close relatives of both sides take part. In reverence to Mother Earth and the departed relatives, as well as by tradition, the food is served and eaten on a table cloth spread on the floor. This is how every Hopi meal was taken as recently as only a few years ago, when Hopi households did not include any noticeable furniture. Through ceremonies, rituals, dancing and feasting, Hopi is truly a continual feast for the eyes and the ears, but especially the heart.

Initiation

The second major event in the life of a Hopi, an event of great ceremonial awakening, is the initiation of boys and girls. The initiation process goes deep into the very fibers of a small but very spiritual group, so that the initiated understand fully what are Hopi essential values.

There are two types of initiation. Every child goes through the first one at the age of ten or twelve, at Powamu time, when the child's godfather gives the child a brand new name. The child is then expected to join one or more of the secret societies. The second initiation guarantees the passage from youth to adulthood and celebrates the event.

For a girl, the second initiation might be called a puberty rite, and it usually takes place at an earlier age than for a boy. The girl starts with a four-day corn grinding ceremony during which time she will be shaded from the sun, as she was just after birth. No meat or salt will be eaten, and on the fifth day, her hair will be ceremonially washed as a symbol of purification. She will be given a new name, and in former times, she would start wearing her hair in the squash-blossom style. Courtship can start after that, as the parents allow a girl to slip out of the house after dark to meet a boy friend. If the girl becomes pregnant but neither the girl or the family feel the boy would be a good choice for a husband and father for the child, the mother will raise her child in her mother's house with the same love and understanding as if she were married.

Around the age of fifteen to twenty, the boy undergoes the second initiation. Part of the Wuwuchim cycle, it emphasizes death and rebirth on a cosmic scale, with a visit to the Underworld as part of a vision quest. When the youth emerges, he is not a boy any longer, but is a man born again at the hands of Spider Woman, the cosmic feminine entity. He will then receive his new name from his grandfather.

Marriage Ceremony

The marriage ceremony is the third major step in the Hopi life cycle, and it is celebrated and ritualized as an essential moment in Hopi life for the bride and groom and for the extended family and the whole of the Hopi people. There is a lot more to it than just the coming together of a man and a woman for the purpose of founding a family. Especially for the bride, keeper of the clans, the marriage ceremony symbolizes the marriage of two individuals with the whole of the community. Because of its symbolic nature as an involvement with the Hopi community as a whole, it can be performed only once, even though the couple might separate or divorce later. If a divorce and a new marriage occur, there would be no ceremony for the second marriage. Marriage is a one-time event, a consecration of being Hopi.

As far as the woman is concerned, the status of a married woman takes the place of another, more evolved type of initiation, the initiation as priestess. The married woman contributes to the welfare of all the Hopi by bringing into the world more Hopi children. Only death will free the married woman of her pledge to the community.

Like a girl's initiation, the wedding ceremony ritual starts with a four-day corn grinding ceremony. The prospective bride grinds the corn in the ancestral way, kneeling in front of a grinding stone in silence and meditation, contemplating the change of status she is about to make. Before this, for weeks and months, the family of the groom have exchanged presents with the family of the bride as a token of their agreement. Piki bread has gone back and forth, and sacks of flour, coffee, and sugar. They are piled in the house of the bride in hundreds.

Then comes the mud fight, in which females of both sides of the family take part. Aunts, mothers, and grandmothers of both the bride and groom gang up on each other in a free-for-all, throwing buckets of mud at each other. Men are caught in the cross-fire. All furniture has been removed from the main part of the house, but it looks like a disaster area. This is the perfect way to use all the pent-up energy accumulated during the months of preparation for the wedding.

On the fifth day, following the corn grinding ceremony, the next ritual is the "hair-washing" ceremony. Using the same bowl, the bride's mother washes the hair of her future son with yucca suds, and the mother of the groom washes the hair of her future daughter. It is done in the presence of close relatives, who contribute to the ceremony by their advice, prayers, and meditation. This purification is followed by the couple presenting themselves to the sun.

At the bride's mother's house, the bride is dressed with close female relatives helping, the men watching. She is dressed in the black ceremonial robe called a "manta," formerly worn by all Pueblo people. She wears white moccasins with white deerskin leggings. The white cotton robes, hand-woven by an uncle in the kiva or his home, are displayed reverently on the bed. She will wear one, and carry the other, wrapped in a mat made of reeds, in her open arms. She will wear the robe she carries when she is called to rejoin her ancestors at the time of her death.

One of the grandmothers arranges her hair in the "married-woman style," with two thick braids wrapped in white cotton thread, and her face is painted white with a special clay.

Then the entire bridal party, all dressed in their finest, are led by the bride, her mother, and her children, toward the groom's house. The men follow with gifts, A nuptial feast takes place there, and hundreds of Hopi attend.

The final ceremonial marriage ritual takes place at the Niman Catsina ceremony when the bride, dressed exactly as she was on the day of her wedding, presents herself alone to the Catsinas and the entire village.

Death and Burial

The ceremony that follows the death of a Hopi is the simplest and shortest of all Hopi ceremonies. The death of a loved one is handled with great reverence; reverence for life leads automatically to reverence for death.

The hair of the deceased is washed in yucca suds, purifying body and soul, and a paternal aunt dresses the male body in his best suit of clothes and puts his favorite turquoise necklace around his neck. In the case of a female, she is dressed in her black manta and white moccasins, then wrapped in the white wedding robe that was woven specifically for that purpose.

The body of the deceased is rubbed with sacred corn meal, the chin blackened, and a string of pahos is placed around the head, flanking a mask made of white cotton called a "white cloud mask." The cloud mask makes the body light enough to float among the clouds, since it will now live in the land of the cloud people. Some piki bread and little pieces of meat are placed with the body so that it will not be hungry during the trip. The body is placed in a sitting position in the grave, wrapped in a blanket. A planting stick is stuck in the grave for the deceased to use to climb to the Underworld and the land of the cloud people.

6 THE UPPERWORLD
AND THE HOPI PROPHECY

The Day of Purification

Long before Pahana, the white man, ever set foot
in the Americas; long before the hegemony of the red race
had been challenged by light-skinned people,
as the prophecies told us it would —
a spot in the immensity of the desert, a center of Spiritual power,
    was Hopi. The land of the peaceful ones.
The continent was different then:
    much space, few to occupy it.

But the energy coming from Hopi is in realms
where communications are not of this world, in dimensions
set by Taiowa and expressed by Massoua,
Hopi was the thread, the bridge,
    the place of peace and balance.

If perhaps there is a name, a word, that can show the world
    what Hopi peace is — it is balance.
The world must grow, expand, but it must do it in balance.
Otherwise, nature, the great regulator, will take over,
as it is now, with floods, eruptions, famine, earthquakes.
This is nature at war, nature that will convince humankind
of the need for balance, to set in motion positive energies
    to reestablish a world in balance.

From the days of discovery to this day, the need to preserve,
unite and insure the balance of the Hopi Way in a pact
made long, long ago between the Great Spirit, Taiowa,
and ourselves, to preserve his way through this bond,
         this promise, to sing the Song of Creation.
And for the rest of the world too —
now that the quality of life is at stake,
in the present days — we must have a model, a plan,
to be followed, to bring at last the peace of ancient days
         through balance of the present ones.
From the beginning, humankind never had more than two ways:
"prayer and meditation," as the leaven of human presence
on Earth. What is seen, touched, and felt is thought to be real,
rather than the reflection of the world of the unseen,
         the real dimension of creation.

In the beginning, we are told, Taiowa, the Creator,
gave us his life plan, as it is written on the rock of Oraibi,
         which we call the prophecy.
If we hold fast to the sacred way as he devised it for us,
what we have gained, we will never lose.
But still, we have to choose between the two ways.
That is the balance of Taiowa's way.
For he will always meet us halfway. That is why on the
sacred petroglyph he is portrayed holding in his hand
the thread of the sacred way. In the other hand is the bow,
for the Bow Clan is the one which led us out of the Underworld
         at the beginning of the Hopi Way.
That is what the arrow shot from the bow means on the rock.
The diagram shows two lines: the lower line
is the path of the Great Spirit, for in its last end, a man is bending
on the cane the old ones use, pointing to the corn,
which is the sacred food that nourished us from the start.

Hopi Prophecy Diagram-Prophecy Rock (Oraibi)

The old one shows he was the first and he will be the last.
And so will we if we hold fast to his pathway.

But next to him, beware of the other way,
the way of life of those who do not pray.
It is easy enough to see that their heads are not fastened
on their body, as it happens with people who use their mind,
instead of their faith in the spirit way.
As Taiowa's life plan shows, their line ends in a zig-zag way,
in the void of the mind of the faithless life
　　　and the fruitless.

But there is another line on the sacred map drawn on the rock
— a vertical line that connects the two ways,
It is like a ladder that some might use to change ways,
to go from the way of peace and balance —
Taiowa's Way, to a path that seems to many a much easier one.

Finally seeing that the Hopi Way of balance is the only chance,
many will choose to climb down the ladder,
to go through the Great Spirit gateway.
This time of confusion, in which many will chose either path,
     is called a time of purification.
So it seems we now are all at this point in our lives,
where indeed purification is for the world, the order of the day.
This is the time, so the Great Spirit says,
where people will earn the name I chose for them: Hopi,
"the people of peace," the name they call themselves today.
The Hopi Way is a condition, a way of life,
and as an elder once said, "Our religion may be of benefit to others."
Indeed it is, for new clans of Hopi are born to teach
     the way of balance,
the Hopi knowledge of peace, the Hopi way.

"Give love to all things, people, animals, plants,
and mountains; for the spirit is one, if Catsinas are many."
The Prophecy says the Earth will shake three times:
first the Great War, then the Second One,
when the Swastika rose above the battlefields of Europe,
to end in the Rising Sun sinking in a sea of blood.
The end of an Empire. . .or perhaps the beginning of another?
Now, what would the third one be?
This, the Prophecy does not say.
For it depends on which path humankind will walk:
the greed, the comfort, and the profit,
     or the path of love, strength, and balance.

When strong-hearted people keep on singing the Song of Creation,
they will find the true path, forgotten by many,
 so Grandpa David says.
When prayer and meditation are used rather than relying
on new inventions to create more imbalance,
 they will also find the true path.
Mother Nature tells us which is the right way.
When earthquakes, floods, hailstorms, drought, and famine
will be the life of every day, the time will have then come
for the return to the true path, or going the zig-zag way.

Long ago, Massoua told us, "Remember the *Pahana*,
the white brother. He has the other stone tablet,
but he has not returned it, yet. He will be sent
so the people who held fast to the Hopi Way can be spared
 from destruction.
He is the purifier, for people to go on with
 the Great Spirit life plan.
It will then open our hearts and minds when a new age
is about to be, with people renewed and purified through fire.
It will be like the pure gold of a new day.
But fire is red, and when it takes command,
it will set the forces of nature in motion.
We will then know purification day has come.
 We all are the caretakers of life.
 The balance of nature depends on us.
 The world will be what we want it to be.

The Hopi know what it should be. They kept the ceremonies
going to help them on the way, and remember what
the sacred path should be: live simply, humbly,
and in a balanced way, for the sake of all that live —
man, animal, plant, rock, and the sacred water.
But man has dropped from the sky the gourd full of ashes.
It boils the sea, burns the land — it indeed is the mystery egg!
It could trigger a rebirth or annihilate us all,
        depending on which way we go.
Purification will come either way.
What will change it all is the Hopi Way.
To help the human race choose its way,
nature will hold its balance. . .
        regardless.
For it has a plan, a grid, a course that has been sowed
        in the beginning.
The great computer, we might say, has been fed
        for all time to come.

So let us hold our breath, and play it right.
On this planet of ours — this "Upperworld,"
as the Hopi would say — no matter how it ends,
        we are all in it together.
How many worlds after this one?
The only issue is the individual choice we make.
When events come at us, is when our life gets its meaning.
This is when we do our best, for it is all we can do
to understand the experiences, good or bad,
        that make our life.

When we leave our own page of history, our best
is all that counts. When the time has come to pack,
and we find no room for all we wanted to take along with us
to the Underworld, our best is all that counts.

THE UPPERWORLD
AND THE HOPI PROPHECY

The first dimension of the Hopi world is the world we all live in, the physical reality of the now. The first five chapters of this book are deeply rooted in other realities, and the Hopi know full well that the "now" must be given an opportunity to manifest itself, that no complete vision of the human or the Hopi experiment can be fulfilled without it.

This vision of the physical reality has always been present in the eyes of the Hopi of the past. Even the mythical and mystical accounts of the first four succeeding worlds vouch for that. These accounts match what modern science has found to have been the common past of all the races that populated the Earth since the beginning of time. Endorsing this story of the past, the Hopi deal with the harsh realities of the present by teaching how to live without resentment or animosity, simply by being. The experiences that people go through trigger the collective reality of the present. Mistakes are being made every day by everyone;

it is a fact of life. But the Hopi know that we are here only to learn.

So, in the clear realism of their understanding of life, they are willing to share their present experience. They have offered to us what is known as the "Hopi Prophecy." It is a composite of the mystical expression of Hopi thought and the historical record of how the Hopi came to be over thousands of years. It is presented in the four successive emergences from the earth. A petroglyphic record on a huge slab of stone called Prophecy Rock is a Hopi version of the Ten Commandments, given to the Hopi as a life plan by the Great Spirit, the giver of life. No one knows how it got there, when and by whom. The monolith stands near the village of Oraibi, perhaps the oldest of all the Hopi villages.

The Hopi Prophecy is an intricate combination of mythical legends and the life plan. It is accepted by most Hopi as the prophetic vision of the Hopi in the development of world events throughout the centuries. This prophetic account by Taiowa, the Creator, offers two plans to the people, the first plan leads to liberation through purification by the ceremonies, and the other follows the path of pleasure, convenience, profit and personal gratification. Developments can be foreseen as either positive or negative depending on the choice of people about which way they follow. Two past wars, the greed of modern society, and what the Hopi call the Gourd Full of Ashes would indicate that the white man has taken the wrong way. The Prophecy foretells another worldwide conflagration and the coming of a powerful world leader called the Purifier.

But essentially, this petroglyphic record points out that from the beginning two obvious plans are offered to mankind. One is leading to a bright future if the desires of the Great Spirit are honored, and the other would eventually lead to the destruction of this world as we know it. This destruction has happened several times before and for similar reasons.

In the text of Chapter 6, the prophecy was spoken by David Monongye; by Dan Katchongva, the departed Chief of the Sun Clan; by Andrew Herequaftewa; by Thomas Banyacya from Oraibi; and by many others.

7 CONCLUSION
AND THE BANANA CLAN

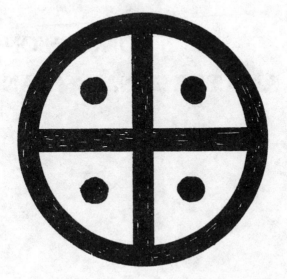

The Life-Plan Symbol

On a hot summer day, around noon, thirty-five years ago, I was lying on a slab of stone, exhausted from working in the fields with my long-time friend and Hopi brother, Leslie Koyawena. The burning sun of mid-day was penetrating my whole body as I lay flat. Some Hopi fields are several miles from the villages, and it was a relief to be napping on this rocky ledge called Soyok Mesa, only a few hundred yards from the village of Shipaulovi, my temporary home. Lying there, I saw a vision, and recounting it thirty-five years later, it still fills me with wonderment.

In the hypnotic twilight that precedes sleep, I distinctly saw the form of a man-like figure. He was incredibly tall, and he did not appear to have any Indian-like features. He had long blond shoulder-length hair.

I said, "Who are you?"

"Somiviki," he replied. And then he said, "You shall have your own clan, which will be named 'The Banana Clan.' " This was thirty-five years ago, and the Banana Clan is a reality today.

Stunned as I was, of course, I reported the incident to the family I was living with at the time. They seemed to grasp what had happened much better than I did, because after a pause, they all burst into loud laughter that still echoes in the village today. The Hopi name for white man is "Pahana," or rather sounds like it, since Hopi is not a written language. This leads to a pun, of course, which is still in the people's minds to this day. A clownish situation, as they saw it, this freshly imported Frenchman telling them of a clan of outsiders wanting to learn to be Hopi.

Hopi clowns drum up incredible situations in order to teach Hopi truths to the people, which made my friends much more prepared to understand this than I was. Looking back, now I know that Hopi prophecies tell of the white brother, the Pahana, who would, one day, come back to the Hopi from the east, bringing with him the brotherly love of the early beginnings. I did not know it then.

The Banana Clan has established itself through the years, and it has entered the fabric of village folklore. Throughout those years, the clan has developed an understanding of the Hopi Way, and it has enriched our lives with a system of values, and a unique philosophy of life.

Meditations With the Hopi, is an attempt to make the Hopi Way available on a soul level to non-Hopis. The secret knowledge of the Hopi is protected, as it should be. There is no need to divulge any of it in order to bring this message. Let us remember that all of us, whites, blacks, reds, or yellows come from the same source and will return to it in the end. It is not surprising that the same knowledge comes to different people in different forms, but in the one most appropriate to each. The Hopi belief in Kwahu, the Eagle Messenger, is a form like the Christ embodied in Christian doctrine. In the Pueblos of the Rio Grande Valley, as in most of Spanish America, the great devotion to the Lady of Guadalupe, an Aztec maiden who appeared to the Indian, Juan Diego in 1531, is another example of inner knowledge coming to people in different forms. It exemplifies the personality of the

Great Mother archetype. Among most Native American tribes, the myth of White Buffalo Woman is another expression of the Great Mother archetype.

No ritual is really the exclusive property of one particular group as long as it can be integrated at the soul or spirit level. There is a human group consciousness which disperses the knowledge as perceived by individuals or groups as a channel to reach the divine. The Hopi Way is one of these ways, and like the Christian, Moslem or Buddhist ways, it will lead the seeker to an understanding of the Creator.

I am concluding *Meditations With the Hopi* with the following anecdotes of my personal experiences as a resident of a Hopi village thirty-five years ago. These experiences made my life fuller, richer, and enabled me to go about the business of living in a more respectful and appreciative way.

The Song of Tawamana*

Oh! Sweet Tawamana,
> you came to us from the shores
> of the rising sun.

Through you we felt the sweet breeze
> of the western wind,
> and the oneness of our white brother, the Pahana.

Some day, he shall bring with him
> the tablet entrusted to him by Massoua
> When he rose from the underworld
> with all of us in search of our land.

Tawamana, you are the swift bird
> that glides into the dark sky of the evening
> when our Sun Father disappears
> behind the San Francisco Peaks
> to start his journey on the other side.

You are the bird that bears
> the sun symbol on its wings.

The thunderbird that goes so fast
> that the eyes of the spirit
> can follow him into the night.

Sweet Tawamana, you brought hopes for the future.
> Remember Hopi, the thunderbird,
> and Tawa, the Sun Father
> that gives us all birth.

May the butterflies of your maiden state
> be with you always.

---

*In the early fifties the author's eldest daughter, then 10 years old, went with him to Shipaulovi, his adopted Hopi village. During their stay, she was given the name Tawamana, the Sun Girl, in a ceremony along with other Hopi girls.

Epitaph to Patsy*

As the mighty eagle is tied on the rooftops
    and dominates the Hopi world
    from its enchained talons;
So also you brought your sacrifice
    to the people,
    the offering of the gift of life.
Enchained, so you were, as your uneven gait
    climbed the ancestral path of stone footsteps
    leading to the ancient village
    on top of the mesa.
Like the eaglet fallen from the nest
    down the precipitous cliff, you had to crawl,
    when others jumped.
In return, the Gods never faltered, offering, in compensation,
    love for the Pahana,
    turning brother into father,
    so you would know love.
From the flowery grave on the sandhill top,
    you smile on your people, the Hopi,
    still you warm my heart,
    keeping your vigil on whites and reds alike
    for us to meet at the twin rocks so near.

---

*During 1949, staying with his adoptive Hopi family at
Shipaulovi, the author asked if he could take Patsy, then 12 years old,
to have her checked by a medical doctor. She had lost one eye to
glaucoma, and she was born with a paralyzed left hip. As a result of
this request, Patsy was given to him as his daughter for the rest of her
life. She died at 45, and now rests on a sandhill overlooking the Hopi
desert.

The Rainmaker*

A thin line of purple light edged the desert toward the Hopi
      buttes, outlining them in the distance,
      almost bordering the Hopi world.
Out of the slumber of the night where they kept themselves
      hidden in the hours of darkness,
      now they were silhouetted in the light,
      a magical background on the stage of Hopi life.
As the oblique light of the rising sun hit them with its first rays,
Leslie and I slipped noiselessly out of the still darkened village,
      racing down the nearly vertical path
      of ancestral stone steps,
      and passing by the kivas,
      we followed the tortuous path to the desert floor.
It was like stepping into a grey shroud,
      this diffused light that precedes the new day.
It was cool on the desert floor, and we had to go swiftly
      to take advantage of it
      to cross the five miles of desert
      separating us from Leslie's cornfield.
Soon, Tawa, the Sun Father, would force us to rest
      under the shade of the willows that grow in the wash.
The sage brush still dewy from the night perfumed the desert
as we went,
      giving it an extra dimension,
      adding to the mystique of unreality.

---

*In late summer, 1949, with my Hopi brother, Leslie Kayawena, we
experienced the above story. This is now an integral part of the
folklore of the village of Shipaulovi, Second Mesa.

In these early hours, magic, mystique and reality are the same.
Leslie carried a little bundle in a red bandana tightened to his
belt; in it he had dry meat and parched corn,
        our meal for the day;
        on his left side a little bag of corn meal
        that never left him.
In his right hand the Hopi rabbit stick,
        ready in case the two long ears of a jack rabbit
        would profile the horizon.
He seemed to be gliding on the sand surface of the desert,
        his moccasined feet almost missing the ground.
Keeping up with him required all my strength.
        I clung to my bow and arrows
        as I ran,
        hoping, like Leslie, to see a rabbit.
We passed fields of corn, melons, squash the size of baseballs—
        the drought had been with us for months.
"This is my cornfield," Leslie said to me,
        pointing at a three hundred square foot place of dry
        sand.
He had not said a word since we left the village.
        Silence is the best teaching of the Indian.
"We need rain. . ."
The wash was nearby, dry of course,
        but underneath the willows, perhaps, a rabbit!
Leslie said rabbits and ground squirrels
        ate his plants.
I was going to try my bow, but I noticed Leslie was sad.
Standing in the middle of his field,
        the palm of his hands facing the heavens,
        his head raised toward the deep blue sky,
        Leslie was praying.

Reaching for his cornmeal, he sprayed the earth, gently. He turned himself toward me and he said: "Shoot one of your arrows so the sun brings rain." I could see he believed in my magic more than I did.

    Leslie knew better.

I cocked the arrow on the bowstring of my sixty-pound aluminum steel bow,
     and aiming straight at the sun,
     I let the arrow fly.
Disappearing from sight, the fleeting arrow
     must have reached its sacred destination:
     it never came to earth again.

Without a word we picked up our hoes and started to push the sand against the corn plants —
     but not for long.
Answering the Hopi prayer, the Cloud People sent us rain. It came down, drenching, at last, the corn and melons so blessed.
     We kept on working.
The earth smelled good, the Hopi Sun God had been good to us. Leslie believed the magical power of the Hopi activated motion
     to bring rain;
     now I believed it too.
The Cloud People, the Catsinas, the God of Heaven and Earth
     had favored us...
It had rained on the parched Earth of the Hopis.

Catsinas

I am Mongwa, the great horned owl Catsina.
    Standing on the highest rooftop
    of our ancient village, Walpi,
    I oversee and regulate the ceremonies.
I move the arms of the giant clock
    as groups of Catsinas move from kiva to kiva,
    according to our ancient rituals.
From the openings in the kiva roofs,
    the ceremonial ladder points to the heavens.
I am not a sorcerer
    and with the magical powers that
    Massoua has entrusted me with
    I keep the groups of Catsinas
    in balance.
Grasping each column of light that
    comes out of the kivas
    in the grip of my talons,
    I move the moon clock so that
    each clan gets in the proper kiva
    at the proper time.
From my sacred perch,
    I see the people
    huddling on the kiva benches.
I see the women and the children
    piled up on the back of the altar.
I see the priest smoking the sacred pipe
    and the children laugh.
Then the ceremony begins
    with the mystical power of Massoua.

Each group of Catsinas moving from kiva to kiva,
    keeping everything in balance.
Then I move the arms of
    the moon clock again
    till way into the night.
Long Hair Catsinas, Supais, Velvet Shirt Catcinas,
    the funny Navajos, the Mixed Catsinas
    stomp their moccasined feet in unison
    on the resounding planks of the kiva floor
    following the rhythm of the big drum
    pounded in sequence by Koyemsi.
The turtle shells make their rasping sound
    along with the deep, resounding vibration
    of the Catsina song.
Gifts of the heavenly visitors
    coming from the Underworld once more.

APPENDIX

POSTSCRIPT

Talking about the ceremonies to a team of officials from Washington, Dan Katchongva, the late Sun Clan leader of the village of Hotevilla who died in 1972 said:

"Any person will benefit by our religious teachings. Our religious orders are the lifeblood of the Hopis. There are many 'religious ceremonies and rites' which deal with the life pattern. This is the very basis upon which we are standing and which we are trying to preserve. As a people who knows these things, we will try to bring this to you in order that you may understand them. These are our authority and forever each leader is walking his stand in carrying on the life of the Hopi people."

GLOSSARY OF HOPI WORDS

AHOLI
Chief Catsina believed to have come into the Hopi Pantheon from preHistoric Central or South America.

ANSAI
Very well.

AZTEC
Small town of western New Mexico in which there is a large Puebloan ruin of the Chaco culture.

BAKABI
Hopi village of third mesa.

CATSINA
Personification of the spirit of a physical entity (animal, plant, person etc. . . .) Can also be written Katchina or Kachina.

CATSINUP
Catsina ceremony or ritual.

CHACO
Historic Puebloan complex comprising several villages in what is now western New Mexico and which gave its name to an entire culture.

CHETTRO KETL
One of the Chaco villages.

CHIMNEY ROCK
Another Chaco complex in Eastern Colorado.

EOTOTO
See AHOLI.

EVAVA
Older brother.

FIRST MESA
Home of four Hopi villages: WALPI, one of the oldest Hopi villages; HANO, settled by TEWA people from the Rio Grande area during the Pueblo Rebellion; SICHOMOVI and POLACCA a more recent one.

HANO
See FIRST MESA.

HEHEYA
Clown Catsina.

HEMIS
A group of Catsinas often participating in the Niman ceremony, believed to have come from Jemez Pueblo in New Mexico.

HILILIS
Warrior Catsina.

HOTEVILLA
A Hopi village of Third Mesa.

HOVENWEEP	Large Puebloan ruin in southern Utah.
KAIBAB	Mountain range and forest bordering the Hopi world to the north.
KIKMONGWI	Traditional village chief.
KISA	Hawk.
KISONVI	Village central plaza.
KIVA	Ceremonial underground chamber.
KOKOPELLI	Seldom seen Catsina dealing with fertility rites.
KOKYANG WHUTI	Spider woman. The all-pervading feminine creative energy. The feminine counterpart of Sotuknang.
KOYAANSQUATSI	Expression to describe a world out of balance.
KOYEMSIS	Also called mudheads. Clownish Catsinas possibly representing an early state of human development.
KWAHU	The Eagle; divine messenger betweeen the Hopis and the creative forces.
KUZ KURZA	Literally, "lost world," possibly what is thought of as Atlantis, or Lemuria . . . and which ended in a global flood.
KYAKOTSMOVI	Also called "New Oraibi." A more recent village housing the offices of the Hopi Council.
LOLAMAI	A Hopi greeting meaning: "all is wonderful".
MASAU	Also MASSOUA or MASAUWI. A god in charge of the Earth who fell into disgrace and was demoted by TAIOWA the creator to become God of the Underworld and the realm of the dead. Was reinstated as protector of the Earth. A myth similar in some ways to Lucifer, the fallen archangel.
MASKI	Literally "corpse house." The place in the Underworld where the spirits of the departed go. By extension means the Underworld.

MATSOP	Second Catsina to appear on the Hopi mesas at the beginning of the ceremonial year after Soyal Catsina. It exemplifies fertility in women and the rest of nature.
MESA-VERDE	Puebloan prehistoric center. Several Hopi clans might have originated there.
MISHONGNOVI	Hopi village of Second Mesa.
MOENCOPI	More recent village. Originally a Hopi farm community attracted by the fertility of the soil of the MOENCOPI wash.
MOTSINI	Mockingbird.
NIMAN	The last Catsina ceremony of the Hopi ceremonial year, usually held in late July or early August depending on the village. Also names "Going-home ceremony," the spirit Catsinas returning to the San Francisco Peaks, their spiritual home.
ORAIBI	Also "Old Oraibi" to distinguish it from New Oraibi (see KYAKOTSMOVI). Possibly the oldest of the Hopi Villages as claimed in myths.
PAHANA	Also Bahana, a white person, but also the mythical white brother of the Hopi who emerged with him from the underworld through the hole of emergence and is due to return to Hopi someday with the sacred tablet he took with him when he left.
PAHO	A ceremonial object of considerable importance made of native cotton and a special type of feather properly consecrated and blessed.
PALATKWAPI	The legendary mythical "Red City of the South." Possibly in Mayan territory where temples and palaces were painted red.
PALONGOHOYA	One of the two sacred twins. A complex myth meaning duality and opposites in the creative realm of things. Common in all Mesoamerican mythology.

PALULUKANG	Guardian Water Serpent spirit.
PAMUYA	The water moon (November, December).
PAVOKAYA	A swift swallow.
PIKAMI	Native ceremonial pudding baked in an earth pit.
PIKI	Ceremonial wafer bread used as an offering in almost all ritual events of Hopi ceremonial or social life.
PLAZA	Spanish word for village square.
POKANHOYA	The other of the two sacred twins. (See PALONGOHOYA).
POWAMU	Important ceremonial cycle during which initiations, the bean dance and the visit of SOYOKO WHUTI, the black ogress, takes place.
POWAMUYA	The purification moon during which the POWAMU ritual takes place. (January-February).
PUEBLO	Spanish word for town or village. By extension name given by the scientific community to the native groups living in such.
PUEBLO BONITO	Literally "The beautiful town". One of the Puebloan complex part of the CHACO CANYON ruins.
QUETZALCOATL	The Plumed Serpent, a major Aztec deity which had great impact on Puebloan mythology.
RINCONADA	A very large kiva at Chaco Canyon, possibly the largest ever built (70 ft. diam.), suggesting that Chaco was once a main religious center.
SHIPAULOVI	A village of Second Mesa.
SHUNGOPOVI	A village of Second Mesa.
SICHOMOVI	A village of First Mesa.

SIPAPU	Also SIPAPUNI or SI-PAH-PU-NAH. Ceremonial opening in the ground symbolizing the hole of emergence through which early humanity emerge into each new created world. Usually to be found on the kiva floor. Also symbolized by the kiva itself, which has a hole at the top, and also by the mythical hole of emergence of all Hopis at the bottom of the Grand Canyon.
SOMIVIKI	Hopi native food resembling a Mexican tamale but stuffed only with blue corn meal and ashes.
SOTUKNANG	Also SOTUKUNANI, sky God and rain God of the Zenith, also nephew of TAIOWA and co-creator of this world.
SOYAL	Second ritualistic event of the ceremonial cycle.
SOYOKO	Also SOYOK WHUTI. Black ogress Catsina surrounded by a whole group of other ogre Catsinas appears on the mesas during POWAMU to remind parents and children of obedience and respect for Hopi beliefs.
SUPAI	A Catsina which originated among the Avasupai, an Indian group living at the bottom of the Grand Canyon.
TAIOWA	Supreme creator, Great Spirit, not a Catsina, the father of the whole of Creation.
TALAWA	New dawn Catsina.
TAWAMANA	"The Sun Girl". A person name.
TAWA MANA	The feminine role of the Sun God.
TAWA TAKA	The masculine role of the Sun God.
TOKPA	Second phase of Creation. Age of the gigantic animals and plants. The age of the Dinosaurs, Diplodocus etc . . .ending by total glaciation.
TOKPELA	The first phase of Creation and solidification of the planet.
TUNGWUP	One of the whipping Catsinas.

TUVKO	Like the English word, "Junior".
KUWA KATSI	Mother Earth, the Goddess of the Earth.
VIRACOCHA	QUECHUA (Inca) word for the Supreme Being.
WALPI	One of the oldest of the Hopi towns on First Mesa.
WUWUCHIM	First of the ceremonial cycles of the Hopi ceremonial year (late November).

ABOUT THE AUTHOR

Robert Boissiere comes to Native American culture through an international odyssey. Born in Paris, France, he narrowly survived the hardship of World War II. He subsequently came to the United States where he followed an inward journey, one which led him to the mesas of Northern Arizona and his adoption by a Hopi family.

Through his continued involvement in Native American culture, Robert Boissiere observes and participates in a tradition which he shares with us in this, his third book.

Other books by the author are *The Hopi Way: An Odyssey* (1985) and *Po Pai Mo: The Search for White Buffalo Woman* (1984).

This book is due on the last date stamped below.
Failure to return books on the date due may result
in assessment of overdue fees.

Fines : $.50 per day